MW00489057

The Charitable Anathema

Dietrich von Hildebrand

The Charitable Anathema

Dietrich von Hildebrand

Roman Catholic Books
P.O. Box 1209 * Ridgefield, Connecticut 06877
BooksForCatholics.com

Copyright © 1993 Alice von Hildebrand

ISBN 978-0-912141-07-7

Table of Contents

Foreword

In the years immediately following the Second Vatican Ecumenical Council, between 1966 and 1976, Dr. Dietrich von Hildebrand prepared numerous articles in which he examined, from a philosophical perspective, a variety of topics related to our knowledge and practice of the Catholic faith, especially with regard to catechesis, doctrine, Sacred Liturgy and Catholic education. These essays were collected under the title *The Charitable Anathema*. Although the articles treat the particular situation in which the Church found herself in the years immediately following the Second Vatican Council, the texts still retain their timeliness, not only because we experience similar challenges in our day, but also because the definitions and clarifications which Dr. von Hildebrand provides have perennial relevance.

Dr. von Hildebrand proceeds in a genuinely philosophical manner by examining various misunderstandings and errors in the understanding and practice of the faith. Central to the philosophical method is the defining of terms, which permits us to know the essence of a given reality, so that we may understand what it is and what it is not. The philosophical practice of making distinctions is essential for us to understand clearly what we believe and practice in the Catholic faith.

As Dietrich von Hildebrand illustrates in the essays, much of the confusion in belief and practice of the faith arises from a failure to understand clearly certain key concepts and their relationships to one another: the relationship between freedom and law; between unity and truth; between charity and communion; between institution and institutionalism; between theoretical and practical authority. He dispels ambiguity by providing accurate definitions of terms and by distinguishing apparently similar realities from one another.

Many of the difficulties that we experience in the life of the Church arise from philosophical problems and from the loss of a sound metaphysics. In the magisterial homily which Joseph Cardinal Ratzinger gave before the Conclave which elected him as Supreme Pontiff, he spoke of a dictatorship of relativism. What Cardinal Ratzinger described is precisely the situation to which Dr. von Hildebrand was responding in the present collection of essays:

> Today, having a clear faith based on the Creed of the Church is often labeled as fundamentalism. Whereas relativism, that is, letting oneself be "tossed here and there, carried about by every wind of doctrine," seems the only attitude that can cope with modern times. We are building a dictatorship of relativism that does not recognize anything as definitive and whose ultimate goal consists solely of one's own ego and desires.

> We, however, have a different goal: the Son of God, the true man. He is the measure of true humanism. An "adult" faith is not a faith that follows the trends of fashion and the latest novelty; a mature adult faith is deeply rooted in friendship with Christ. It is this friendship that opens us up to all that is good and gives us a criterion by which to distinguish the true from the false, and deceit from truth. ("Homily of His Eminence Card. Joseph Ratzinger, Dean of the College of Cardinals," 18

April 2005, *L'Osservatore Romano*, weekly edition in English, 20 April 2005, p. 3.)

Relativism—the loss of a sound metaphysics and consequently of a sense of an objective reality—is indeed the greatest danger in our days. It leads to a great many errors that destroy persons and society.

To be a herald of the truth, the Christian must be able to think deeply and correctly about the fundamental human questions and the questions of faith. While it is not necessary for each person to become a philosopher, in the totally secularized society in which we live it is imperative for each believer to develop a philosophical habitus, to become philosophical, so that he has clearly in his mind important definitions and distinctions which permit him to judge well what is proposed to him as truth by the society at large. The philosophical habit permits man to consider all things under the aspect of the objective order which God has placed in Creation and, above all, inscribed in the human conscience, and which He has restored in the Redemptive Incarnation.

Dr. Dietrich von Hildebrand was devoted in the study of truth taught to us by both faith and reason, and in the life of truth through love of God, the source of all truth and the giver of both faith and reason. For that reason, it is most fitting that the collection of essays in *The Charitable Anathema* includes some of his essays about the Sacred Liturgy. In the time since the Second Vatican Ecumenical Council, though not because of the teaching of the Council, there has been an exaggerated attention to the human aspect of the Sacred Liturgy, which has overlooked the essence of the Sacred Liturgy as the encounter of God with us by means of sacramental signs, that is, as the direct action of the glorious Christ in the Church to give to us the grace of the Holy Spirit.

When he writes of the Sacred Liturgy, Dr. von Hildebrand does not tire of emphasizing the theocentric character of the liturgical action and the proper response of deep reverence before the action of God. It is as critical today as it was half a century ago to devote attention to the truth that the Sacred Liturgy is centered in God, that it is, in fact, the action of God the Son Incarnate, seated in glory at the right hand of the Father and at the same time active in the Church on our behalf for the salvation of the world.

It is my hope that the republication of the essays of Dr. von Hildebrand will make the fruit of his philosophical and theological labors better known in the Anglophone world. I am convinced that the reader will find the various essays published in the present volume a trustworthy guide to navigate the difficult times in which the Church finds herself today.

Raymond Leo Cardinal Burke
September 12, 2017
Feast of the Holy Name of Mary

I

The Charitable Anathema

It is as much a crime to disturb the peace when truth prevails as it is a crime to keep the peace when truth is violated. There is therefore a time in which peace is justified and another time when it is not justifiable. For it is written that there is a time for peace and a time for war and it is the law of truth that distinguishes the two. But at no time is there a time for truth and a time for error, for it is written that God's truth shall abide forever. That is why Christ has said that He has come to bring peace and at the same time that He has come to bring the sword. But He does not say that He has come to bring both the truth and the falsehood.—Blaise Pascal

Never has the fatal danger of irenicism been more acutely identified than in these words of the great French thinker Blaise Pascal. In our own day, no less than in his, the valuing of unity over truth plays a central role in the crisis of the Church; for the Church of Christ—the Holy, Roman, Catholic, Apostolic Church—is based on this fundamental principle: the absolute primacy of divine truth, which is the very primacy of God. It is the principle lying at the basis of the condemnation of all heresies in the course of the past 2000 years, the basis of all anathemas, the Church's very *raison*

1

d'être, the rationale for all her apostolic and missionary work. The Church has survived because she has always condemned errors. In the words of Cardinal Newman, "the fear of error is simply necessary to the genuine love of truth."

A spirit very different from Newman's reigns in the Church today. In the face of a fearful crisis menacing the Church—a crisis of faith, a crisis from within—we hear the argument, even from some bishops, that the most regrettable thing today is disunity among Catholics. I have heard this argument before.

When I was living in Austria before the Second World War, there was a Catholic professor of philosophy in Vienna who continually made novenas for the Nazification of Austria. I was his radical opponent, and he fought against the anti-Nazi review I was then publishing. Once the Archbishop of Salzburg, a rather mediocre, jovial man, but kind and very friendly, approached me and suggested that I should make peace with this professor. He argued that it was so important that Catholics should not fight each other, that there should be unity and peace among Catholics. I replied: "I have no personal feud with him, but if he professes false theories, which are incompatible with Christ, then I feel obliged in my conscience to fight him. One cannot make peace at the cost of truth, and especially not at the cost of divine truth. This would imply an offense of God." Unfortunately, he did not understand my argument. "But professor," he said, "you are, after all, a friendly man; make peace with him—the important thing is that there be no split between Catholics...."

Fight for Truth

No. A far more important thing is that there be no Catholics—no priests, no lay people, no bishops—who profess

2

heresy, who profess theories incompatible with the deposit of Catholic faith. The fact that many orthodox Catholics fight these heresies is not deplorable; on the contrary, we should rejoice that there still are faithful Catholics, and that they raise their voices against heresies, for God expects that of them. St. Paul says there always will be heresies and he adds that God permits them to test the faithful. The disunity that is based on the incompatibility of truth and falsehood cannot and should not be avoided. "It is as much a crime to disturb the peace when truth prevails as it is a crime to keep the peace when truth is violated."

To deplore disunity as such, instead of deploring heresies, instead of condemning these and calling them by their name, implies first of all that one would keep unity even at the cost of truth. But, of course, true unity presupposes unity in truth. Error, falsehood, can never be the basis for true unity. That holy, supernatural unity of which our Lord speaks in the priestly prayer *ut unum sint*—that all may be one—can come to pass only in the profession of divine truth, in the membership of the Mystical Body of Christ. It is a unity which includes some but, by the same token, excludes others. As Father Werenfried van Straaten reminds us, "Jesus' prayer 'that all may be one'...may not be separated from His other words: 'I say unto you that whoever does not enter by the door of the sheepfold is a thief and a robber...I am the door!'" The same principle is expressed in the first encyclical of Pope Pius XI: *Pax Christi in regno Christi,* the peace of Christ in the reign of Christ.

Even on the natural level, unity that is not grounded in truth is either a very silly or a very dangerous thing. That shallow comradeship so typical of modern society, for example, in which we approach everyone regardless of his relation to God in a spirit of "tolerance"—the spirit incarnated in the words of Frederick II of Prussia: "Let everyone attain beatitude in his own fashion"—that is a foolish pseudo-unity lacking any common principle to truly unite men.

Such "togetherness," however, can be worse than foolish; it can be a sinister force when it is based not on a lack of principle, but on a common error—on an idol. The togetherness found in Nazism or in Communism is an amazing thing. Devotion to the common idol goes so far that the devotees are ready to die for it. So many young Germans gave their lives in the war while screaming, "Heil Hitler!" They had given themselves, in unity, to the devil.

Now there is certainly a natural unity which has value— for example, the unity found in marriage, even among pagans, and the unity of the family. This unity is primarily based on natural love—on an affinity of souls. But for such a unity to transcend the merely natural, it must be cemented in a unity of conviction. Even in a marriage, or in the family, unity can be secondary to truth. Thus Christ said: "Do not suppose that I have come to bring peace to the earth; it is not peace I have come to bring, but a sword. For I have come to set a man against his father, a daughter against her mother...." The truth of Christ, that is, must be preferred even to familial peace.

If we are truly concerned for unity among Christians, I submit that there is only one way to restore it, and it is the time-honored way: the anathema against all heretics. This is the way the Church has survived, kept her identity, through all centuries. This is the way, most recently, by which the holy Pius X of glorious memory saved the unity of the Church: by his unequivocal condemnation of heretics, by his introduction of the oath against modernism for all priests, he liberated the Church from the thralldom of modernism.

True unity can be restored only by the conversion of the heretic—or at least his submission—or by his excommunication.

At this point, of course, we must take account of the disuse into which the anathema has fallen in recent times. The reluctance to use this indispensable tool of the Church's authority is a consequence of the unfortunate irenicism popular today among Catholics; and that irenicism, I believe, is in turn the consequence of a basic confusion between charity and communion.

Communion and community presuppose a common end, a union in truth. Christian communion presupposes a union in His holy Church. Charity, on the contrary, does not presuppose common acceptance of the true faith. The obligation of charity extends to *every* human being, even to the enemies of God. It actually demands more of us than communion does. It requires an ardent love of Christ, a full personal I-Thou relation with Christ, so that our heart is melted by Christ; but it *presupposes nothing* on the part of the neighbor to whom our charity is directed. Communion, on the other hand, presupposes far less on our part than charity does, but a great deal *more* on the part of the one with whom we enter into communion. Religious communion presupposes that the other person shares our faith.

It is because of this confusion between charity and communion that the anathema is considered hard and uncharitable. The anathema excludes the one who professes heresies from the communion of the Church, if he does not retract his errors. But for precisely this reason it is an act of the *greatest charity* toward all the faithful, comparable to preventing a dangerous disease from infecting innumerable people. By isolating the bearer of infection, we protect the bodily health of others; by the anathema, we protect their spiritual health. And did Christ not say that we should not fear those who kill the body, but fear him who has power to cast into hell?

And more: a rupture of communion with the heretic in no way implies that our obligation of charity toward him ceases.

No, the Church prays also for heretics; the true Catholic who knows a heretic personally prays ardently for him and would never cease to impart all kinds of help to him. But he should not have any communion with him. Thus St. John, the great apostle of charity, said: "If any man say, I love God, and hateth his brother; he is a liar." But he also said: "If any man come to you, and bring not this doctrine, receive him not into the house...."

Hand in hand with this confusion of charity and communion there has been a diluting and softening of charity in the minds of many so-called liberals or progressives. They confuse that victorious and holy charity of which St. Paul speaks in Chapter XIII of his first Letter to the Corinthians with a mere humanitarian benevolence. They no longer see that charity can live in our hearts only as the fruit of our love of Christ. Thus we often hear the nonsense that we could learn true charity from the atheists: we Catholics, the line goes, love only God and the atheists only man, so we must combine with them to reach true charity; and to accomplish this the Church must leave her "ghetto" and acquire an openness to the world.

Protect the Truth

Now this use of the term "ghetto" is very illustrative of the mentality of irenicism. If it is meant to imply simply that there was much bureaucratism in the Church, and that it should be done away with, so as to overcome the prevalence of merely conventional Catholicism—then it is certainly praiseworthy to hope the Church will break out of the ghetto. (It ought to be more widely recognized, though, that bureaucratism is an evil which can never be ousted by laws—that is, by more bureaucracy, but only by the renewal of faith and the love of Christ.) But it is a disastrous error to apply this term "ghetto" to the fortress of truth. It is a sign of the divine character of the Church, a sign that she is not a merely human institution, that she pitilessly bars the door to all error, to all heresies, to all defections from the deposit of Catholic faith. Through all the turmoil of human error, against the rhythm of historical ups and downs, the Church for 2000 years has remained untarnished by dogmatic error. The history of the Church is nothing less than testimony to a miracle: never surrendering to the onslaught of heresies, never succumbing to the weakness and sinfulness of many prelates, even popes, never compromising with error, the glorious fortress of divine truth has remained impregnable. It requires an incredible mediocrity to look at this historical miracle and see...a ghetto! It is the mediocrity of the followers of intellectual fashion, those of whom Kierkegaard spoke: "Philosophy sheds a skin with every step it takes, and the stupid follower crawls into it!"

Teach the Truth

Many of the followers are currently wrapped tight in the skin of a false ecumenism which is another manifestation—perhaps the most significant of all—of the age's crippling irenicism.

The term "ecumenism," properly understood, has to do with the Church's universality, one of her essential marks. It belongs to the essential mission of the Church to strive to convert every human being.

In contradistinction to the Jews, who do not ordinarily seek conversions because they consider the revelation of God in the Old Testament as directed exclusively to a Chosen People, the Catholic Church follows the command of Christ: "Teach ye all nations, baptizing them in the name of the Father and of the Son and of the Holy Ghost." This is why she is called the *Catholic* Church, from the Greek word meaning "universal."

But that ecumenism which has become fashionable since Vatican II is something quite different; in some interpretations it even contradicts true Catholic universality.

Every true Catholic should see in every non-Catholic person, in every man who is not yet a member of the Mystical Body of Christ, a catechumen *in spe,* a convert in hope. The prayer of Christ, *ut unum sint,* looks to the conversion of every individual person to the true Church. But a union which results from a melting together of different religious communities, instead of the conversion of the individual to the Catholic Church, is a very different thing.

Today it would seem to make *practical* sense only in the case of the Orthodox Church, which is not heretical but only schismatic. At least in principle, recognition by the Orthodox of the primacy of the Roman Pontiff would suffice to restore unity. Thus every gesture of love and every manifestation of a deep communion between the Holy Father and the head of the Orthodox Church is a practical and hopeful step toward a return of the Eastern Church to the unity which existed undisturbed until the ninth century.

With respect to Protestants, however, obstacles to union are far more numerous and far more serious—so much so that the hope of *corporate* reunion with the Protestant sects is probably illusory, and certainly fraught with grave danger. The emphasis of Vatican II is not really on ecumenism, as that word is properly understood; what the Council urges is actually a new attitude toward non-Catholic religions. The Council invites Catholics, while clearly recognizing the dogmatic errors of the sects, to recognize also what is true in them.

By this recognition it is hoped that Catholics will feel not only our dolorous separation from our Christian brethren, but also the imperfect unity resulting from those truths which we share with them.

This is certainly a noble and praiseworthy thing; but it is also, I repeat, a dangerous thing. For compared to the Church's universality, and the mission of conversion we must all feel as a consequence of it, the recognition of what we have in common with non-Catholics is a quite secondary consideration. I know that these words violate fashionable ecumenical etiquette, but Pope Paul VI himself in his first encyclical, *Ecclesiam Suam*, clearly stressed the different degrees of unity we have with non-Catholic religious communities, and the differing attitudes we must have toward them. Firstly, our separation from the Protestants is based on fundamental dogmatic differences—and the differences vary from sect to sect. Secondly, we are faced not only with the many different denominations, but also with divisions within denominations, most of which have different and entirely independent leaders in different countries. So no matter how numerous and how sincere our gestures of love and fellowship toward the leaders of the sects, we can have little hope of the collective return of an entire denomination to the sheepfold.

And here, of course, is the source of the danger: the possibility that as the excitement of the "ecumenical spirit" continues, without bringing true spiritual union, it will lead us to emphasize the elements which we share with the sects *at the cost of* those elements in which we differ. Here again we would commit the basic error of placing unity over truth. And it would be the worst illusion of true unity, a mere apparent unity, at the expense of precious elements of our deposit of faith, at the expense of a disfiguration of the holy Church, a watering down of her liturgy, a bashful covering of the cult of the Virgin, an embarrassed avoidance of mentioning the saints.

Irenicism, it can truly be said, covers a multitude of errors. In discussing some of them—the temptation to value unity over truth; the distortion of the true meaning of unity which irenicism can lead to; the reluctance to protect the Church by condemning heresies and anathematizing heretics; the confusion of charity and communion; the degeneration of irenicism into mediocrity and pursuit of the fashionable; the corruption of the ecumenical spirit into a kind of Rotarian mentality in religious garments—in discussing all of these fruits of irenicism, I have not been able to hide from myself that every one of them is very much a clear and present fact. The Catholic Church today is visited with each of these plagues.

There is, in other words, no reason whatever for optimism; therefore let our hope grow in proportion! For the Lord God has said, and still repeats to us today:

Et portae inferi non praevalebunt.

II

"Modern Man" and the Voice of Authority

Is it really true that authority—especially the authority of office—no longer has an important place in matters spiritual and moral? Must its exercise be so reticent, so diluted with discretion and caution and fear of provoking reaction, that it scarcely can be seen for what it is? There are many who believe that the democratic trend of our time has created a general antipathy—not to say rebellion—against constituted authority of all kinds. They say, for example, that the attitude of the young renders authority in education irrelevant.

We are not referring to those who believe that authority is something evil, but rather to those who are convinced that political, social, educational, familial and, above all, religious authority has largely lost its efficacy for the man of today. They conclude that the only valid and efficacious expression authority can take when faced with errors, moral deviations and even rebellion is that of the loving mother who with great patience and hope tries to lure her wayward children back to truth or moral integrity. Concretely, this attitude results in tolerance of the most unorthodox opinions and behavior and continuous "discussions," unresolved and vague. At the present time in the Catholic Church there are persons holding responsible office—bishops and religious superiors—who share this view of the changed situation of authority today.

There are two false judgments at work here which must be examined in turn: first, that authority is in fact so unpopular that it has become inefficacious—incapable of asserting itself effectively, of commanding assent in virtue of its place and function in the structure of a community; second, that it follows that a conciliatory, patient, tolerant, solicitous—indeed, passive attitude is the only appropriate one those in authority can adopt toward deviations and deviators.

On the first thesis we shall make three points.

It is always dangerous to assume that a given epoch is characterized by a strict uniformity of mental posture. Although an attitude may be widespread to the point of dominance, we should recall that historical epochs always include many different tendencies, some mutually opposed. And the most that one could say today is that authority is widely unpopular, that rebelling against authority is rather fashionable. But it is a massive oversimplification to assert that authority will not command respect from many men in our time.

Moreover, it is a mistake to believe that the disrespect for authority today represents a new independence of mind. In reality, our time is marked by a blind yielding to thoughtless slogans and a flight to pseudo-authorities. The multiplicity of secular ideologies, quasi-mythological cults—such as scientism, Freudianism, progressivism, evolutionism, nationalism, epochalism, various forms of relativism—proves that many Catholics are replacing the free and conscious submission to the true authority of the Church with an unreflective submission to pseudo-authority, an abdication of reason in the name of reason.

And if we are not drugged by the myth of a "new," a "modern" man, we shall see that in his depth, in his fundamental weaknesses and strengths and needs, in his profoundest aspirations and desires, in his essential being, man remains the same. And the need for authority is rooted deep in man's psyche; ultimately, it flows from his creatureliness. Behind the apparent unpopularity of authority lies hidden a deep longing for authority. Those who consider protests against authority a sign of man's "coming of age" are either in ignorance or arrogance—exalting rebellious pride, moral sloth and adolescent insecurity.

Thus, protest against authority is not the only attitude manifested today; the real situation is the rivalry between traditional authority and new pseudo-authorities; the need for authority is fundamental and inescapable.

As for the second thesis: it by no means follows that authority today must embrace a rather passive role.

In the first place, we must distinguish between palatableness and efficacy. Palatable it has never been for man's fallen nature to acknowledge lawful authority. Obedience always contains an element of self-abnegation (although it should result in a superior self-fulfillment). But it is a psychological oversimplification to conclude that authoritative interpositions are therefore inefficacious.

In the second place, although an unassertive authority may be appropriate in certain realms and relations, it is definitely wrong in others. In education, for example, while authority has often been abused, it is neither possible nor desirable to eliminate its active exercise. (Recently, we have had dramatic proof that when educational authority abdicates, education stops.) Of course, parents are by their very nature an authority for the child, and it is their duty to use their position to command and forbid, to answer the child's need and desire for enforced decisions about what is right and wrong. It is undoubtedly true that parental authority should be permeated with love, patience and respect for the inestimable worth of the child's soul; but love and authority are co-necessary: a love without a firm authority is irresponsible and, finally, destructive. And with regard to the political realm, it should not be necessary to insist on the legitimate role of forceful authority, for only anarchists would deny it.

Now, although authority must inevitably be enforced by coercion in the realms of education and the State, this is neither legitimate nor efficacious in persuading someone of the truth. No one has the right to attempt to impose a conviction by coercion. Coercion is here forbidden; authority nonetheless remains. The intellectual and moral stature of a person—of a teacher, for example—can legitimately and efficaciously play a certain role in the formation of convictions—although it can never replace understanding and insight.

This applies all the more in the realm of faith. In the "Declaration on Religious Freedom" of the Second Vatican Council, the use of coercion in matters of religious faith has been thoroughly condemned. Faith cannot and should not be coerced; it is a grace, a gift from God. (This in no way diminishes the obligation to respond to the offer of God's grace and adhere to the true faith. But that is another question.)

However, because religious authority should not express itself in coercion, it does not follow that it is not to be energetically exercised in other ways. The Catholic Faith, as such, implies that those who have been given the grace to hold it surrender to the authority of the Holy Church, that they believe and accept and assent to its infallible magisterium. The authority of the Church in spiritual matters, in the government of the Church and in the definition and teaching of the Faith, derives from its divine institution, from the fact that Christ entrusted to the Apostles and their successors under the Pope the preaching of the divine revelation and its protection from the infiltration of error.

Thus, the Church is authoritative in its essential mission, and it belongs to the exclusive competence of the Church to decide whether a given doctrine is heretical or orthodox. Anyone who believes that he can decide this question for himself and is free to adhere to or interpret doctrine according to his arbitrary lights can no longer be considered a Catholic.

Because it is the divinely-willed mission of the Church to distinguish heresy from orthodoxy in order to safeguard the integrity of the *depositum fidei*, it follows that the Church can never permit an alleged unpopularity of authority to inhibit it from defining the truth and, correlatively, locating and denouncing error. The efficacy of the authority of the Church depends on the divine will that ratifies its exercise, not on the extent of its popularity in a given epoch.

To suggest that the anathema (which is the clearest expression of authority and most called for when confusion is greatest) should be *replaced* by a patient and loving admonition is to ask the Church to shirk its mission.

Furthermore, not only can disrespect for authority have no influence whatever on the Church's mission openly and unequivocally to defend the integrity of the Faith, but also the Church's loving concern for those large numbers of the faithful who do respect and love her holy authority and need her guidance and protection will require her to issue public, emphatic and specific warnings about false doctrine and false prophets. It is likely, of course, that a theologian or teacher or journalist who is spreading heretical thought will resent the anathematizing of his opinions; it is indeed quite possible that, instead of obediently yielding to the Church's authority (in the divine institution of which he is supposed to believe), he may rebelliously cling to his heresies. But the millions of innocent and faithful Catholics will know with absolute certainty the identity of heretical opinions and will thus be protected from infection.

Many of the faithful are not equipped to know whether a new theory is in harmony with the authentic doctrine of the Church. They believe in the infallible magisterium of the Church and want to be orthodox Catholics, but cannot by themselves judge whether Teilhard de Chardin's theories, for example, approach heresy or are dangerous to faith or morals. The mission of the Church is to move quickly to protect the purity of faith of the great body of faithful, rather than to hesitate for fear of the reaction of heretical or irresponsible theologians, pastors, teachers and journalists. And the fact that something has been unequivocally condemned by the Church as contrary to the Faith will mean as much to the faithful as it has ever meant.

So much for the question of the Church's authority to promulgate true and condemn false doctrine, to identify heresy. But what of the correlative question of how to deal with the *persons* who are spreading false or dangerous opinions among the faithful? Here, there are two pastoral concerns in response to two themes or situations: the concern for the prevention of the spread of evil; and the concern for the restoration of the heterodox speculator to his due subordination to the magisterium of the Church. Quite simply, the community will first want the police to prevent the arsonist from setting fires, *then* it will be solicitous for his chastisement and rehabilitation.

In the presence of dangerous opinions, the first duty of a bishop (or the superior of a religious order or the head of a school or university) is to the faithful under his care: he will silence a heretical priest or remove an unorthodox teacher. *Only* when a man is not in a position to poison the minds of the innocent faithful can authorities in the Church afford to modify their disciplinary measures in a way calculated to ease his return to orthodoxy and fidelity.

And is it not a strange contradiction of the very nature of the priesthood—and even more, of a religious order—which requires a vow of holy obedience, for a bishop or religious superior to declare that he can no longer forbid a priest under his supervision to spread heretical views because that would be an authoritative approach unsuited to our "modern age"? What government today would hesitate to remove an ambassador or public official who uttered views that were opposed to its policies? And in the Church something infinitely higher is at stake—the faith of Catholics and a priest's holy mission. If the bishop or superior does not intervene to prevent the spread of corruption, he is fully responsible for any resulting injury to souls.

No one coerces a man into the priesthood or a religious order. And no one forces him to remain. A priest freely promises to say nothing incompatible with the doctrines of the Church and to obey the order of his bishop or superior. It implies not the slightest disrespect for his freedom and dignity to require him to submit to the authority of the Church. If he has lost his faith, if he wishes to assert his own judgment against that of the authorities, then he is free to leave his order or the priesthood or even the Church. No coercion will prevent his departure. (It is to sponsor the most blatant hypocrisy to argue, as the Jesuit Avery Dulles did [*America*, October 28th, 1967], that a priest can deny the doctrine of the Church and still "belong with us," that bishops must be unusually patient with "reputable theologians" who, for example, "deny...that Jesus was conceived without the cooperation of a human father." Fr. Dulles is urging authority to accommodate those who want to be in the Church and out of it at the same time, who wish to deny the

Faith without relinquishing the privileges and prerogatives of membership in it.)

Today, with so many heretical and dangerous and confusing "new opinions" abroad, the faithful must hope—and, if necessary, they must demand—that their bishops and others in authority in the Church fulfill their strict obligation to protect their flocks by silencing or suspending those who are spreading heresy and error. Ecclesiastical authorities must not confuse the personal spiritual problems of wayward Catholic speculators with the public problem of the effect of their speculations.

However much the spiritual directors of these men might have to take into account individual psychology—however suitable a patient, subtle approach might be in individual cases—the action of authority cannot be determined by them, but rather by the needs of the faithful who are exposed to heresy and error and who require from authority, therefore, its open, clear, firm and concrete exercise.

III

The Institutional Church
and Institutionalism

It is a largely unmarked irony of our time that many of those who are most vociferous in their criticism of the "preconciliar Church" are themselves fostering a most dangerous form of the very thing Vatican II was designed to correct. Let us examine, for example, how those who attack the Church as an institution, as a complex, highly articulated organization, are often responsible for the perversion of *institutionalism*.

The Fathers of Vatican II envisioned a renewal in which every practice of the Church and its members would be permeated with the spirit of Christ, with the stream of supernatural life. They wished to overcome a certain ossification, a certain bureaucratism and legalism, that had crept into the pastoral and administrative life of the Church. This institutionalism was the result of a secularist mentality. Whether it takes the form of a relaxing into the world or an abuse of authority, or the reading of doctrine as a program for worldly enterprise, the spirit of the world may indeed creep into the sanctuary of the Church. And the councils are always concerned with the perversion of the institutions of the Church into mundane forms.

19

But in this "postconciliar age" there are a number of prelates and writers who—in the name of Vatican II!—are propagating the opposite of what the Council intended: a thoroughgoing secularization. At times they exemplify the bureaucratism and abuses of authority they pretend to deplore; more generally, they oppose a new form of secularization to the old. In both cases they remain dominated by the antithesis of the spirit of Christ—secularism; for moral laxity, legalism and bureaucratism, and the naturalization of dogma (which we see more and more today) are all deviations stemming from the same moral source. However much, on the surface, they may seem opposed, and however much, on the personal level, they suggest different temperamental and psychological tendencies, they are equally manifestations of man's fallen nature.

Legalism consists in neglecting the spirit and adhering only to the letter. It is an overemphasis on what is juridically accessible at the cost of moral values. It approaches all moral commandments as if they were positive commandments; and it approaches the positive commandments of God and His Holy Church as if they were profane laws.

The secularism of legalism and bureaucratism appears, for example, when more emphasis is placed on disciplinary obedience than on orthodoxy and moral integrity. If a bishop does not intervene effectively when a theologian or teacher is spreading heretical speculations or when a priest is inventing new rites for holy Mass, but immediately suspends a priest for a disciplinary infraction, he is putting a higher value on institutional discipline than on his apostolic mission. This is institutionalism, properly so called.

Both a breakdown of discipline through yielding to worldly interests and an emphasis on discipline at the expense of fidelity to the spirit of the Gospel are betrayals of the institution Christ founded. The holy authority of the

Church is based on the fact that the Church is a divine institution, that it possesses an infallible magisterium, and that, therefore, all of its defined dogmas are valid and true. If the Church were merely a human institution, if the deposit of Catholic faith could be transformed in the course of history, the religious authority of the institutional Church would lose its basis. Thus, the legitimacy of disciplinary loyalty is undermined whenever, through laxity or immanentism, the Church as an institution is detached from faith in her divine foundation or whenever the articles of faith are doubted or "re-interpreted."

The attack on the institutional Church that various "progressives" are making today is a much more dangerous error than carelessness in conforming to ecclesiastical discipline. The attack on the Church as an institution is in essence an attempt to separate the material and organizational life of the Church from the supernatural life that informs it. This amounts to a deliberate secularization on behalf of some disembodied "invisible" Church.

It belongs to the glorious perfection of the supernatural community of the Roman Catholic Church that it be simultaneously the Mystical Body of Christ and a concrete, formal society; that its inner life of a community of grace find a clear exterior expression embracing canon law and the administrative structure of the Church. It is a fundamental ontological principle that the higher the rank of a community the more its inner life achieves organic expression in a formal society. This is the case in marriage, as it is in the religious order—above all, in the Church. It is quite wrong to oppose the "juridical" or "institutional" church to the "church of charity" as many of our "progressive" theologians are fond of doing. But the necessity and glory of the institutional Church can be understood only if one is not blind to its divine character. For what is actually a wonderful organic efflorescence of the superabundant supernatural life of the Church—something essentially linked to its holy mission—becomes merely a mundane institution characterized by the profane, secular failures of legalism and bureaucratism and power politics when juridical acts are separated from their supernatural foundation. The institutional Church is a great gift for which the faithful should thank God. But as soon as it is stained with the spirit of secularism, the self-assertion of the corrupted part of the Church becomes institutionalism—a deformation of the Church's incarnate life.

Those who decry the institutional Church, who regard it as an irrelevant accretion, are thus doing the most to bring about institutionalism. Moreover, these same persons exhibit a tendency to interpret the faith with a view to accommodating it—under the banner of *aggiornamento*—to the relativistic, secularist mentality of our time; and this is the very thing that will deprive the structure of the visible Church of all validity or legitimacy. In former times, the secularization we have termed "employeeism," which is seen in the mentality of those priests who recognize merely a disciplinary loyalty to a bishop, produced a harmful ossification in the Church. But today we can observe a new growth of this institutionalism in those who no longer consider the bishops successors of the Apostles, but rather mere functionaries of a human institution—presiding officers of assemblies of religious sects, or executive officers of a kind of religious parliament—men designated to carry out the will of the "People of God." Indeed, there seem to be bishops who so conceive of their role. And these prelates, who have more or less accepted the "new theology" (and thereby betrayed the *depositum Catholicae fidei*), often exhibit a bureaucratic legalism and clerical authoritarianism—the most obvious features of institutionalism—in their treatment of priests and laymen who refuse to compromise with the spirit of the world.

IV

Belief and Obedience:
The Critical Difference

Is it true, as a certain Father Virgilia Levi charged recently in
L'Osservatore Romano, that the defenders of the encyclical
Humanae Vitae are now contradicting themselves by express-
ing their deep concern over the new *Missale Romanum?* Do
Catholic orthodoxy and filial submission to the Vicar of
Christ require one to hail every practical decision of the Holy
Father? What should be one's inner attitude toward practical
decisions of the Pope, decisions that seem ill-advised or
dangerous in their consequences or even decisions that seem
to compromise with the spirit of secularism?

Such questions increasingly preoccupy Catholics striving
to defend the true doctrine of the Church against the onslaught of today's innumerable heresies. In order to answer
them, in order to understand the nature of the authority of
the Church, we must, from the very beginning, clearly distinguish between *theoretical* and *practical* authority.

Theoretical authority is a guarantee of the truth of a
statement. In the natural, human realm we find only relative
theoretical authorities. We accept the truth of a generally
admitted scientific discovery—the existence of cosmic rays,

for instance—although we ourselves are not able to verify it and still less capable of grasping it as we grasp an evident fact. What is learned in a school or university, and is not intelligible in itself (as is, for instance, the fact that two plus two is four) is learned only through acceptance of the teacher's theoretical authority. But, obviously, this authority is only a relative one: many scientific "truths" once universally accepted have subsequently been discredited. It would be unreasonable not to accept what such a theoretical authority teaches—it would even be foolish—but we know, nevertheless, that this authority is not infallible, and thus is relative.

There is but one *absolute* theoretical authority: the Church in matters of faith and morals. It is a basis of our Catholic faith that Christ has entrusted His divine revelation to the Holy Church and that the Church under the guidance of the Holy Spirit is infallible in matters of faith and morals—that she is an absolute theoretical authority in these matters.

It is because of this absoluteness that we are obliged—even morally obliged—to accept the Church's word as true, to believe in it; whereas to accept the word of human, natural—*relative*—theoretical authority is never obligatory. Not to accept it may be unreasonable, but it is not morally evil. And obviously belief in the teachings of the Church has the character of faith—that is, an unconditional, solemn clinging to her teaching; whereas all belief in natural theoretical authorities is a mere natural conviction and differs radically from an act of religious faith.

Practical authority, on the other hand, appeals not to belief—to the acceptance of a truth—but to obedience. We are obliged to obey an authentic practical authority and to submit to its commandments. Whereas no natural theoretical authority is obligatory, there are true and binding *practical* authorities in the natural realm. Such is the authority of the parents over the child; such is the authority of the state. The Church is a practical authority of a higher order, because here the partial representation of God has a sacred character. It is a sacred authority and, in all matters which belong to her realm of competence, her commandments and administrative measures have a solemn and morally binding character.

Thus we can see that the theoretical authority of the Church appeals to our belief, while the practical authority of the Church appeals to our obedience. Clearly, then, the infallibility of the Church applies only to the Church as a theoretical authority.

Now, obviously, the essence of infallibility implies that there are never any contradictions between a formerly defined dogma and a new authoritative declaration *de fide*. At the moment such a contradiction came to pass, the infallibility of the Church would explode, would have been proved a mere illusion on our part. Other possibilities do not exist. New dogmas may differentiate and explain former dogmas, they may complement them, they may refer to something which has never been defined before but was implicit in the faith or its logical consequences, or in any case does not contradict a former dogma. But no dogma, once authoritatively taught, can ever be authoritatively denied. For instance, the rejection of Luther's *sola fides* theory could never be superseded by an affirmation of Luther's theory. The consequence would be a collapse of the Church's infallibility.

In what concerns the practical authority of the Church, her positive commandments, the question of infallibility simply does not apply. A positive commandment, an administrative measure, or any prescription cannot be true or false but only valid or invalid, good or evil, useful or useless. Truth is never the theme in the positive commandments or laws of any practical authority. If in a particular state the voting age is reduced from 21 to 18, we may find the measure wise or unwise, felicitous or disastrous, but it makes no sense to call it true or false. This applies also to the practical authority of the Church. When a pope introduces changes in canon law, or when he splits one diocese into two, or permits children to receive communion at an early age, or changes laws of fasting, it may be felicitous or unfortunate, it may be more adequate than a former law or less adequate—but questions of infallibility and of truth are irrelevant.

The history of the Church offers innumerable examples of changes made according to decisions of the practical authority of the Church; often, but not always, the authentic spirit of the Church—that is, the spirit of Christ—motivates her to revoke a former prescription and to introduce an opposite one. In this case we are bound to obey the prescription or commandment; we should accept it with the respect due it—but we are not obliged to find it felicitous. We can regret it and pray that it may be again revoked.

Now, even though there are differences in the required attitudes of the faithful Catholic to the theoretical and the practical authority of the Church, we must emphatically stress that there are important links between the two authorities. First, the practical authority of the Church *presupposes* the Church's theoretical authority. The practical authority of the Church is different from that of parents, of a judge, of a minister of state, of a policeman. We can with our reason grasp the legitimacy or illegitimacy of their claim to a natural, practical authority; but all practical authority in the Church, and above all that of the Supreme Pontiff, has its roots in *faith*, in the divine institution of the Church, in her supernatural character, in the infallibility of her theoretical authority. Thus as soon as one loses faith in the absolute, theoretical authority of the Church, as soon as one no longer believes in her infallibility in matters of faith and morals, as soon as one begins to speak of a pluralism of dogmas and no longer

26

believes in the divine institution of the Church—at that moment the practical authority, all disciplinary authority of the Church, loses its foundation. A bishop, for instance, who adopted the theories of certain modern theologians who replace the infallible teaching of the Church with a Hegelian world-spirit evolving in history, would by this assumption undercut the basis of his own authority; if this assumption were correct, his episcopal authority would be a ludicrous show.

The second link between the theoretical and practical authority of the Church is that any disciplinary action of the Church that would, in its effect, contradict any dogmatic truth of the *depositum Catholicae fidei*, or any moral teaching of the Church, would be invalid. If a pope were to abolish auricular confession, for example, his commandment would be doubtful in its validity because it would be incompatible with a canon of the Council of Trent concerning the sacrament of Penance.

On the other hand, all manifestations of the practical authority that are by their very nature necessary consequences of a dogma or a moral teaching of the Church are beyond all possible changes and are absolute in their validity. Thus the practical authority has an extremely wide range, reaching from fundamental canon laws down to measures that refer to momentary situations—an interdict, for example, or the promotion of an individual prelate.

Having briefly analyzed, then, the relations between the Church's theoretical and practical authority, let us turn to the different responses required of the faithful to manifestations of the two authorities.

In the case of the theoretical authority, the important question is whether a teaching refers to matters of faith and morals and does not contradict the deposit of Catholic faith. Here infallibility is in question, when a teaching is pronounced *ex cathedra* or *de fide*. A specific case may help to illuminate the matter.

The Second Vatican Council solemnly declared in its Constitution on the Church that all the teachings of the Council are in full continuity with the teachings of former councils. Moreover, let us not forget that the canons of the Council of Trent and of Vatican Council I are *de fide*, whereas none of the decrees of Vatican II is *de fide;* the Second Vatican Council was *pastoral* in nature. Cardinal Felici rightly stated that the Credo solemnly proclaimed by Pope Paul VI at the end of the Year of Faith is from a dogmatic point of view much more important than the entire Second Vatican Council. Thus, those who want to interpret certain passages in the documents of Vatican II as if they implicitly contradicted definitions of Vatican I or the Council of Trent should realize that even if their interpretation were right, the canons of the former councils would overrule these allegedly contradictory passages of Vatican II, because the former are *de fide,* the latter not. (It must be stressed that any such "conflict" would be, of course, apparent and not real.)

Our belief in the teachings of the Church *de fide* must be an absolute and unconditional one, but we should not imagine that our fidelity to the Church's theoretical authority is satisfied merely by acceptance of *ex cathedra* pronouncements. We also must adhere wholeheartedly to teachings of the Church in matters of morality, even if they are not defined *ex cathedra*. The teaching of the encyclical *Humanae Vitae,* for example, is binding because its content has always been part of the teaching of the Church; in it we are confronted with the theoretical authority of the Church embodied in the tradition of the ordinary magisterium. It is not a mere practical commandment of the Church, like the commandment to go to church on Sunday. It is a statement about a moral fact; that is, it states a *truth:* that birth control is sinful.

It is forbidden not because of the Pope's policy, but because the theoretical authority of the Church declares its sinfulness. Here, as in all cases of a teaching of the theoretical authority, the old maxim applies: *Roma locuta: causa finita.*

The situation is different when positive commandments of the Church, practical decisions, are at stake. Here we are not faced with the infallible Church. While we must obey such decisions and submit to them in reverence and deep respect, we need not consider them felicitous or prudent. Here the maxim *Roma locuta: causa finita* does not apply. If we are convinced that any practical change or decision is objectively unfortunate, noxious, compromising, imprudent, or unjust, we are permitted to pray that it may be revoked, to write in a respectful manner about the topic, to direct petitions for a change of it to the Holy Father—to attempt, in a variety of ways, to influence a reversal of the decision.

A late friend of mine, Marc Sangnier, had a marvelous attitude about these matters. He was the first prominent French Catholic in the beginning of this century to endorse the French Republic, when most of the faithful and all of the bishops were ardent royalists. Sangnier founded a religious movement called *Sillon*, "furrow." It was a movement filled with an admirable religious ardor—most of the members went every night for hours to adore Christ in the Church of *Sacre Cœur* in Paris. The movement grew quickly, and the bishops were full of suspicion, because members of *Sillon* were all republicans and fought the royalist *Action Française*. Certainly it was not free of dangerous confusions; some of its members uttered doubtful ideas. But Sangnier himself was an exemplary, orthodox Catholic, highly esteemed by Pius X. When that great, holy Pope wrote a letter to Sangnier expressing his wish that he submit his movement to the bishops, Sangnier immediately sat down and wrote to the

Holy Father: This is the greatest moment in my life—the moment in which I can show my love and my devotion to the Holy Church. I wish to serve the Church not as I intend, but as she wants it. The *Sillon* is dissolved.

In this heroic spirit he dissolved an organization to which he had dedicated his life for many years and to which he had given a great part of his private fortune. But he then founded a new association called *Jeune Democratie* in which he continued to propagate his social ideals based on a deep Catholic faith; but it was an entirely secular organization which could by its very nature not fall under the jurisdiction of the French bishops.

The papal commandment to submit the *Sillon* to the bishops implied a great personal sacrifice for Sangnier, but it was a response to several audacious, even heretical statements of young members of the organization, which at the time of the great danger of Modernism called for papal intervention. That the motives of the bishops were more of a political character when they drew the attention of the Pope to the *Sillon* does not change the fact that this authoritative suggestion of Pope Pius X was a normal protection of orthodoxy.

Quite different circumstances surrounded the practical decision of Pope Clement XIV, who, under the pressure of several European monarchs, dissolved the Jesuit order in 1773. Nobody could doubt the orthodoxy and filial devotion of those Catholics who disapproved of this compromise of the Pope, regretted it, and prayed, or even worked, for a revival of the order. They were finally successful when Pope Pius VII restored the Jesuit order in 1914.

The point, of course, is that obedience to the practical disciplinary decisions of the pope does not always imply approval of them. When such a decision has the character of compromise or is the result of pressure or the weakness of the individual person of the pope, we cannot and should not say: *Roma locuta: causa finita.* That is, we cannot see in it the will of God; we must recognize that God only permits it, just as He has permitted the unworthiness or weakness of several popes in the history of the Church.

Today, many theologians propose to replace the deposit of Catholic faith with their own subjective opinions about Christ, His virginal birth, His resurrection, and so on. This is not only clear apostasy, but also the most ridiculous presumption—as if, in matters of faith, their subjective opinions could have any weight. Theologians like Schillebeeckx or Metz cannot base their theologizing about Heaven and Hell and redemption on any real knowledge, because these mysteries are not accessible to any natural knowledge or research. But obviously the same is not true of disciplinary orders or enactments of a pope. They are not only not infallible, but we can with our reason grasp the eventual injustice or inadequacy of them. If we think, for instance, of the excommunication that Pope Gregory XI launched against all Florentines because the Republic of Florence joined a war against the pontifical state—according to this decision all Florentines were outlawed and could, without any claim to redress, be made slaves; no one was bound to keep his word to them or pay any debts owed to them; no one could trade with them or help them in any way whatever—all the princes of Christendom were called to arms to exterminate them— we can clearly grasp its morally doubtful character

Similarly, I cannot deny that I deeply regretted the Concordat of the Holy See with Hitler's Germany under Pius XI, which was signed in April 1933. I believed then that this Concordat would confuse many Catholics in Germany and would never be taken seriously by the Nazis. Unfortunately, events proved that I was right.

Nor can I conceal—and here we are returning to the point from which we started—the fact that the new *Missale Ro-*

manum seems to me an incomparably greater mistake than that Concordat. I share the view of the great, venerable Cardinal Ottaviani—a true rock of orthodoxy—and of the group of Roman theologians who authored a critical study of the "new" Mass for Cardinal Ottaviani, that this liturgical innovation implies a contrast, at least by omission, with the *de fide* canons of the Council of Trent about the Mass.

On account of my deep love for and devotion to the Church, it is a special cross for me not to be able to welcome every practical decision of the Holy See, particularly in a time like ours, which is witnessing a crumbling of the spirit of obedience and of respect for the Holy Father.

But we cannot close our eyes to the fact that the rubrics of the new *Ordo* (as distinct from the text itself) are at variance with the definition of the essence and *raison d'être* of Holy Mass as given by the Council of Trent. Consequently it must be feared that in their sermons, many priests will be encouraged to emphasize the character of the "assembly of the people of God" at the cost of both the mystery of the sacrifice of the Holy Mass and the ineffable gift for every individual soul granted in the sacrament of the Eucharist—faith in which is already menaced by certain heretical trends rampant in the Church.

Are theocentrism, the most intimate communion of the individual with Christ in the Eucharist, the reality of the glorious union with the saints, the militant, suffering and triumphant Church, recollection and reverence—are all these truths fostered in the new Ordo as securely as in the old? And are not these precisely the truths that need to be emphasized at the present moment?

We must not overlook the fact that behind many of the deplorable phenomena of our times—promiscuity, the rapid spread of criminality, student rebellion—there lurks a deep despair which echoes a cry for redemption, the ever-present longing of the *anima naturaliter Christiana* for Christ, the Epiphany of God, in His full supernatural glory. The unique character of our time calls not for yielding to the secular spirit—that can only increase the current despair—but for the full disclosure of the glory of the *depositum Catholicae fidei.*

Thus I hope and pray that the Tridentine Mass will not be abolished, but will continue to be celebrated side by side with the new Ordo. Furthermore, I hope and pray that in the course of time, its superiority, from the pastoral as well as the doctrinal standpoint, will be recognized by the Holy See, and that in the future the Tridentine Mass will be reinstated as the official liturgy of the holy Mass in the Western Church.

The present situation of the Church and the duty imposed by that situation on all faithful Catholics resembles more the time of Arianism in the fourth and fifth centuries, or the time of Luther and Calvin, than it resembles the situation of the Church from 1846-1958, the period of the great pontificates of Pius IX, Leo XIII, Pius X, Benedict XV, Pius XI and Pius XII. In this latter period there was no revolution inside the Church; even when the cancerous heresy of Modernism arose, it was unequivocally condemned and overcome by the great Pius X, the embodiment of charity and humility, but a lion as soon as orthodoxy was threatened.

In this long period, so condemned by today's "progressives," all faithful Catholics were accustomed to unlimited confidence in the practical decisions of the Holy See. The situation of the Church did not demand that all the faithful who understood the dangers of the time heed the call to fight for orthodoxy—as the faithful were called in the time of Arianism. But ours is, I believe, the period of the greatest crisis the Church has ever faced, a period in which the anathema has become unpopular and is unfortunately considered as incompatible with charity, in which authority is discredited and many prelates do not use their authority to discipline priests who are teaching heresies. In such a period, every faithful Catholic who is fully devoted to Christ, to the teaching of the Church, to the deposit of the Catholic faith, to the dogmas, is called to raise his voice in defense of orthodoxy. In the first line of defense, naturally, are the orthodox bishops and priests; but the orthodox layman is also called.

Our unconditional submission to the theoretical authority of the Church, because Our Lord has entrusted to it His divine revelation, manifests itself primarily in our faithfulness to the deposit of Catholic faith. Let us, as we answer the call to defend orthodoxy, reflect on the glorious history of the Church. Let us take faith from the fact that no pope has ever proclaimed anything heretical, anything contrary to the deposit of Catholic faith; and let us also recall the innumerable graces flowing from the Church into the souls of the faithful throughout the centuries. Let us remember the innumerable saints to whom the Church has given birth. Let our hearts be filled with ardent love for the Church, the Bride of Christ. But when this love inevitably fills our hearts with deep sorrow over a practical decision imposed on us—which we cannot but think unfortunate and dangerous in its consequences—let us not fall into despairing confusion. Let us realize that it would be disastrous to identify the God-willed response of faith to the infallible theoretical authority of the Church with the completely different response of obedience to the practical authority of the Church. Though we must obey such a practical decision, we must not approve it; nay, we must even pray for its revocation, and, in full respect, strive with all legitimate measures to persuade the Holy Father of its danger, all the while proclaiming wholeheartedly: *Credo in unam sanctam catholicam et apostolicam ecclesiam!*

V

The Case for the Latin Mass

The arguments for the new liturgy have been neatly packaged, and may now be learned by rote. The new form of the Mass is designed to engage the celebrant and the faithful in a communal activity. In the past the faithful attended Mass in personal isolation, each worshipper making his private devotions, or at best following the proceedings in his missal. Today the faithful can grasp the social character of the celebration; they are learning to appreciate it as a community meal. Formerly, the priest mumbled in a dead language, which created a barrier between him and the people. Now everyone speaks in English, which tends to unite priest and people with one another. In the past the priest said Mass with his back to the people, which created the mood of an esoteric rite. Today, because the priest faces the people, the Mass is a more fraternal occasion. In the past the priest intoned strange medieval chants. Today the entire assembly sings songs with easy tunes and familiar lyrics, and is even experimenting with folk music. The case for the new Mass, then, comes down to this: it is making the faithful more at home in the house of God.

Moreover, these innovations are said to have the sanction of Authority: they are represented as an obedient response to the spirit of the Second Vatican Council. This is said notwithstanding that the Council's Constitution on the Liturgy goes no further than to *permit* the vernacular Mass in cases where the local bishop believes it desirable; the Constitution plainly insists on the retention of the Latin Mass, and emphatically approves Gregorian chant. But the liturgical "progressives" are not impressed by the difference between permitting and commanding. Nor do they hesitate to authorize changes, such as standing to receive Holy Communion, which the Constitution does not mention at all. The progressives argue that these liberties may be taken because the Constitution is, after all, only the first step in an evolutionary process. And they seem to be having their way. It is difficult to find a Latin Mass anywhere today, and in the United States they are practically nonexistent. Even the conventual Mass in monasteries is said in the vernacular, and the glorious Gregorian is replaced by insignificant melodies.

My concern is not with the legal status of the changes. And I emphatically do not wish to be understood as regretting that the Constitution has permitted the vernacular to *complement* the Latin. What I deplore is that the new Mass is *replacing* the Latin Mass, that the old liturgy is being recklessly scrapped, and denied to most of the People of God.

I should like to put to those who are fostering this development several questions: Does the new Mass, more than the old, stir the human spirit? Does it evoke a sense of eternity? Does it help raise our hearts from the concerns of everyday life—from the purely natural aspects of the world—to Christ? Does it increase *reverence*, an appreciation of the sacred?

Of course these questions are rhetorical, and self-answering. I raise them because I think that all thoughtful Christians will want to weigh their importance before coming to a conclusion about the merits of the new liturgy. What *is* the role of reverence in a truly Christian life, and above all in a truly Christian worship of God?

Reverence is of capital importance to all the fundamental domains of man's life. It can be rightly called "the mother of all virtues," for it is the basic attitude that all virtues presuppose. The most elementary gesture of reverence is a response to being itself. It distinguishes the autonomous majesty of being from mere illusion or fiction; it is a recognition of the inner consistency and positiveness of being—of its independence of our arbitrary moods. Reverence gives being the opportunity to unfold itself; to, as it were, speak to us; to fecundate our minds. Therefore reverence is indispensable to any adequate knowledge of being. The depth and plenitude of being, and above all its mysteries, will never be revealed to any but the reverent mind.

Remember that reverence is a constitutive element of the capacity to "wonder," which Plato and Aristotle claimed to be the indispensable condition for philosophy. Indeed, irreverence is a chief source of philosophical error.

But if reverence is the necessary basis for all reliable knowledge of being, it is, beyond that, indispensable for grasping and assessing the values grounded in being. Only the reverent man who is ready to admit the existence of something greater than himself, who is willing to be silent and let the object speak to him—who opens himself—is capable of entering the sublime world of values.

Moreover, once a gradation of values has been recognized, a new kind of reverence is in order—a reverence that responds not only to the majesty of being as such, but to the specific value of a specific being and to its rank in the hierarchy of values. And this new reverence permits the discovery of still other values.

Man reflects his essentially receptive character as a created person solely in the reverent attitude; the ultimate grandeur of man is to be *capax Dei*. Man has the capacity, in other words, to grasp something greater than himself, to be affected and fecundated by it, to abandon himself to it for its own sake—in a pure response to *its* value. This ability to transcend himself distinguishes man from a plant or an animal; these latter strive only to unfold their own entelechy. Now: it is only the reverent man who can consciously transcend himself and thus conform to his fundamental human condition and to his metaphysical situation.

The irreverent man, by contrast, approaches being in an attitude either of arrogant superiority or of tactless, smug familiarity. In either case he is crippled; he is the man who comes so near a tree or building he can no longer see it. Instead of remaining at the proper spiritual distance, and maintaining a reverent silence so that being may speak its word, he obtrudes himself and thereby, in effect, silences being.

In no domain is reverence more important than religion. As we have seen, it profoundly affects the relation of man to God. But beyond that it pervades the entire *religio*, especially the worship of God. There is an intimate link between reverence and sacredness: reverence permits us to experience the sacred, to rise above the profane; irreverence blinds us to the entire world of the sacred. Reverence, including awe—indeed, fear and trembling—is the specific response to the sacred.

Rudolf Otto has clearly elaborated the point in his famous study, *The Idea of the Holy*. Kierkegaard also calls attention to the essential role of reverence in the religious act, in the encounter with God. And did not the Jews tremble in deep awe when the priest brought the sacrifice into the *sanctum sanctorum*? Was Isaiah not struck with godly fear when he saw Yahweh in the temple and exclaimed, "Woe is me, I am doomed! For I am a man of unclean lips...yet my eyes have seen the King"? Do not the words of St. Peter after the miraculous catch of fish, "Depart from me, O Lord, because I am a sinner," testify that when the reality of God breaks in upon us we are struck with fear and reverence? Cardinal Newman has shown in a stunning sermon that the man who does not fear and revere has not known the reality of God.

When St. Bonaventure writes in *Itinerium Mentis ad Deum* that only a man of desire (such as Daniel) can understand God, he means that a certain attitude of soul must be achieved in order to understand the world of God, into which He wants to lead us.

This counsel is especially applicable to the Church's liturgy. The *sursum corda*—the lifting up of our hearts—is the first requirement for real participation in the Mass. Nothing could better obstruct the confrontation of man with God than the notion that we "go unto the altar of God" as we would to a pleasant, relaxing social gathering. This is why the Latin Mass with Gregorian chant, which raises us up to a sacred atmosphere, is vastly superior to a vernacular Mass with popular songs, which leaves us in a profane, merely natural atmosphere.

The basic error of most of the innovations is to imagine that the new liturgy brings the holy sacrifice of the Mass nearer to the faithful, that shorn of its old rituals the Mass now enters into the substance of our lives. For the question is whether we better meet Christ in the Mass by soaring up to Him, or by dragging Him down into our own pedestrian, workaday world. The innovators would replace holy intimacy with Christ by an unbecoming familiarity. The new liturgy actually threatens to frustrate the confrontation with Christ, for it discourages reverence in the face of mystery, precludes awe, and all but extinguishes a sense of sacredness.

What really matters, surely, is not whether the faithful feel at home at Mass, but whether they are drawn out of their ordinary lives into the world of Christ; whether their attitude is the response of ultimate reverence; whether they are imbued with the reality of Christ.

Those who rhapsodize on the new liturgy make much of the point that over the years the Mass had lost its communal character and had become an occasion for individualistic worship. The new vernacular Mass, they insist, restores the sense of community by replacing private devotions with community participation. Yet they forget that there are different levels and kinds of communion with other persons. The level and nature of a community experience is determined by the *theme* of the communion, the name or cause in which men are gathered. The higher the good which the theme represents, and which binds men together, the more sublime and deeper is the communion. The ethos and nature of a community experience in the case of a great national emergency is obviously radically different from the community experience of a cocktail party. And of course the most striking differences in communities will be found between the community whose theme is supernatural and the one whose theme is merely natural. The actualization of the souls of men who are truly touched by Christ is the basis of a unique community, a sacred communion, one whose quality is incomparably more sublime than that of any natural community. The authentic *we-communion* of the faithful, which the liturgy of Holy Thursday expresses so well in the words *congregavit nos in unum Christi amor,* is possible only as a fruit of the *I-Thou communion* with Christ Himself. Only a direct relation to the God-man can actualize this sacred union among the faithful.

The communion in Christ has nothing of the self-assertion found in natural communities. It breathes of the Redemption.

It liberates men from all self-centeredness. Yet such a communion emphatically does not depersonalize the individual. Far from dissolving the person into the cosmic, pantheistic swoon so often commended to us these days, it actualizes the person's true self in a unique way. In the community of Christ the conflict between person and community that is present in all natural communities cannot exist.

So this sacred community experience is really at war with the depersonalizing "we-experience" found in mass assemblies and popular gatherings which tend to absorb and evaporate the individual. This communion in Christ that was so fully alive in the early Christian centuries, that all the saints entered into, that found a matchless expression in the liturgy now under attack—this communion has never regarded the individual person as a mere segment of the community, or as an instrument to serve it. In this connection it is worth noting that totalitarian ideology is not alone in sacrificing the individual to the collective; some of Teilhard de Chardin's cosmic ideas, for instance, imply the same collectivistic sacrifice. Teilhard subordinates the individual and his sanctification to the supposed development of humanity. At a time when this perverse theory of community is embraced even by many Catholics, there are plainly urgent reasons for vigorously insisting on the sacred character of the true communion in Christ.

I submit that the new liturgy must be judged by this test: Does it contribute to the authentic sacred community? Granted that it strives for a community character; but is this the character desired? Is it a communion grounded in recollection, contemplation and reverence? Which of the two— the new Mass, or the Latin Mass with the Gregorian chant—evokes these attitudes of soul more effectively, and thus permits the deeper and truer communion? Is it not plain that frequently the community character of the new Mass is purely profane, that, as with other social gatherings, its blend of casual relaxation and bustling activity precludes a reverent, contemplative confrontation with Christ and with the ineffable mystery of the Eucharist?

Of course our epoch is pervaded by a spirit of irreverence. It is seen in a distorted notion of freedom that demands rights while refusing obligations, that exalts self-indulgence, that counsels "let yourself go." The *habitare secum* of St. Gregory's *Dialogues*—the dwelling in the presence of God—which presupposes reverence, is considered today to be unnatural, pompous, or servile.

But is not the new liturgy a compromise with this modern spirit? Whence comes the disparagement of kneeling? Why should the Eucharist be received standing? Is not kneeling, in our culture, the classic expression of adoring reverence? The argument that at a meal we should stand rather than kneel is hardly convincing. For one thing, this is not the natural posture for eating: we sit, and in Christ's time some reclined. But more important, it is a specifically irreverent conception of the Eucharist to stress its character as a meal at the cost of its unique character as a holy mystery. Stressing the meal at the expense of the sacrament surely betrays a tendency to obscure the sacredness of the sacrifice. This tendency is apparently traceable to the unfortunate belief that religious life will become more vivid, more existential, if it is immersed in our everyday life. But this is to run the danger of absorbing the religious in the mundane, of effacing the difference between the supernatural and the natural. I fear that it represents an unconscious intrusion of the naturalistic spirit, of the spirit more fully expressed in Teilhard de Chardin's immanentism.

Again, why has the genuflection at the words *et incarnatus est* in the Credo been abolished? Was this not a noble and beautiful expression of adoring reverence while professing the searing mystery of the Incarnation? Whatever the intention of the innovators, they have certainly created the danger, if only psychological, of diminishing the faithful's awareness and awe of the mystery.

There is yet another reason for hesitating to make changes in the liturgy that are not strictly necessary.

Frivolous or arbitrary changes are apt to erode a special type of reverence: *pietas*. The Latin word, like the German *Pietaet*, has no English equivalent, but may be understood as comprising respect for tradition; honoring what has been handed down to us by former generations; fidelity to our ancestors and their works. Note that *pietas* is a derivative type of reverence, and so should not be confused with primary reverence, which we have described as a response to the very mystery of being, and ultimately a response to God. It follows that if the content of a given tradition does not correspond to the object of the primary reverence, it does not deserve the derivative reverence. Thus if a tradition embodies evil elements, such as the sacrifice of human beings in the cult of the Aztecs, then those elements should not be regarded with *pietas*. But that is not the Christian case.

Those who idolize our epoch, who thrill at what is modern simply because it is modern, who believe that in our day man has finally "come of age," lack *pietas*. The pride of these "temporal nationalists" is not only irreverent, it is incompatible with real faith.

A Catholic should regard his liturgy with *pietas*. He should revere, and therefore fear to abandon the prayers and postures and music that have been approved by so many saints throughout the Christian era and delivered to us as a precious heritage. To go no further: the illusion that we can replace the Gregorian chant, with its inspired hymns and rhythms, by equally fine, if not better, music betrays a ridiculous self-assurance and lack of self-knowledge.

Let us not forget that throughout Christianity's history, silence and solitude, contemplation and recollection, have been considered *necessary* to achieve a real confrontation with God. This is not only the counsel of the Christian tradition, which should be respected out of *pietas;* it is rooted in human nature. Recollection is the necessary basis for true communion in much the same way as contemplation provides the necessary basis for true action in the vineyard of the Lord. A superficial type of communion —the jovial comradeship of a social affair—draws us out onto the periphery. A truly Christian communion draws us into the spiritual depths.

Of course we should deplore excessively individualistic and sentimental devotionalism, and acknowledge that many Catholics have practiced it. But the antidote is not a community experience as such—any more than the cure for pseudo-contemplation is activity as such. The antidote is to encourage true reverence, an attitude of authentic recollection and contemplative devotion to Christ. Out of this attitude alone can a true communion in Christ take place.

The fundamental laws of the religious life that govern the imitation of Christ, the transformation in Christ, do not change according to the moods and habits of the historical moment. The difference between a superficial community experience and a profound community experience is always the same. Recollection and contemplative adoration of Christ—which only reverence makes possible—will be the necessary basis for a true communion with others in Christ in every era of human history.

VI

Positive and Negative Thinking

Perhaps never before has there been as much intellectual fraud as there is today. In the mass media—and even in discussions on university campuses—this intellectual fraud appears chiefly as the manipulation of slogans designed to bluff the hearer or reader, and prevent him from thinking clearly. For a typical example, let us consider how the terms *positive* and *negative* are now most often used to discredit the refutation of pernicious errors and to give credit to the most shallow speculations.

The intellectual swindlers who play such an important role in public discussions will often denominate as "positive" propositions and attitudes they favor. They thereby seek to forestall questions of truth and value by enveloping their prejudices in a vague suggestion of "creativity," "originality," "openness," "unaggressiveness." This is the device of the cuttlefish. The moment one tries to grasp it, it emits a murky substance to confuse and deceive.

In reality, the popular slogan usages of *positive* and *negative* is a distortion of the genuine meanings of the terms. In proper usage they can refer to existence and nonexistence or to value and disvalue. They can refer to desirability and undesirability, or to answers to questions and demands, or to results of tests and inquiries. But when these terms are applied to attitudes of mind or to theses—by way of suggesting an evaluation—an intellectual fraud is committed; for they are then being used to evoke vague associations that distract from the question that alone matters—namely: Is this attitude objectively called for? Or: Is this thesis true?

To judge an attitude without consulting the object to which it refers is to ignore the question of relevance. And to praise an assertion or approval for being "positive," or to deride a denial or criticism for being "negative," tells us nothing about the truth of the affirmed thesis or the denied proposition. A true proposition should be asserted; a false proposition, denied or refuted. An attitude adequately responsive to the object in view should be recommended; one inappropriate to the object, rejected or criticized.

The same principles apply to the sphere of action. We cannot characterize an action as "good" and a decision not to act as "bad" until we know whether the situation objectively calls for action or for refraining from action. In view of the cult of activism that is flourishing today, it is desirable to emphasize this point: not only is it just as necessary and just as morally good to abstain from evil as it is to perform a good action, but it is also as much a real response—just as "positive"—as any other morally good action. (One thinks of the temptation of Joseph by Potiphar's wife.)

Moreover, to abstain from sinning (which is motivated by love of God) is not only as "positive" as any other good action, but is even our *first* duty—one that takes precedence over the accomplishment of an action that brings forth good. Likewise, to reject or refute an error is as valuable and desirable—as "positive"—as to affirm or discover a truth.

It is the nature of truth to exclude every contradiction of itself. Thus, the rejection of errors and falsehoods can never be separated from the affirmation of truth. The one implies the other.

To give the impression that affirmations are "positive" and denials "negative" is to misrepresent completely the nature of judgments and propositions. This abuse of the language transforms the terms *positive* and *negative* into deceptive slogans and thus amounts to an intellectual swindle.

It is against the background of the foregoing analysis that we must evaluate the criticism that has been made of the document on doctrinal errors that was presented to the synod of bishops by a preparatory commission under Cardinal Browne. This document stressed the necessity of isolating and expelling from the Church the false doctrines that are now being proclaimed within it. Some laymen and priests, availing themselves of the facilities of both the Catholic and the secular press, termed the document something "merely negative" and implied that the Synod should rather be concerned with "positive" tasks. A flood of similar remarks appears nowadays whenever the Holy Father attempts to expose heretical opinions and warn the faithful about them.

Now, the deposit of Catholic faith is the revelation of Christ passed on by the Apostles and not—as a number of "positive-thinking" Catholic writers seem to assume—the reflection of a *Weltgeist* unfolding itself in history. It follows that the sacred mission of the Holy Church to announce divine revelation, to spread the message of Christ, is indissolubly linked to the condemnation of heretical speculations and heretical interpretations of dogma. Christian revelation inevitably requires of the Church that it reject a doctrinal error as soon as this error is propagated.

As a matter of fact, the process of the differentiation and ever more explicit formulation of Christian revelation has always, during the two thousand years of Christianity, gone hand in hand with the refutation of errors and heresies. And the apostolate of the Faith has always been accompanied by the anathema pronounced against heretical teachings. This is quite clear in St. Paul, as well as in all the councils—from the First Nicaean to the First Vatican. Moreover, Pope Paul VI has declared that no previous anathema was suspended by Vatican II; and in the Dogmatic Constitution on the Church we find the Council Fathers declaring their intention to follow faithfully the teachings of previous councils.

The intellectual swindle implicit in the slogans *positive* and *negative*—their spurious and counterfeit quality, the intention to brainwash, to undermine clear thinking—is especially apparent in the attitude of those busy Catholics who call themselves "progressives." They are quick to denounce the condemnation of heresies as something "negative." They try to give the impression that they favor the Church's becoming broadminded, open, tolerant. "Why always criticize?" they say. "Why always stress the danger out of fear? Is this not a negative attitude? Let us rather be positive; let us stress what is true in these new theories and opinions, instead of negatively emphasizing imperfections and hunting for heresies. Let us take an optimistic approach, instead of fretting about dangers. Let us be positive as we renew and modernize the Church."

Yet these "positive-thinking" progressives are brimming over with criticism of the Church.

When it comes to the "Church of yesterday" (which somehow is still around today), they shed their sheep's clothing and proffer judgments that express contempt and scorn for the history of the Church. They cannot decry the Church enough for her "narrowness," her "lack of charity," her past "triumphalism" (another fraudulent slogan) and her present "out-of-dateness." This irreverent, unjust (for they do not hesitate to falsify the record) and prejudiced criticism of the

Church is considered to be—not "negative," but "constructive" and "positive."

This inconsistency makes it clear that these terms are slogans—verbal weapons—and have nothing to do with rational analysis. They belong in the same class as the slogans of German National Socialism, Communism and the other mass movements and ideologies that attempt to evade the tests of truth and value.

VII

The Meaning of Vatican II

The extent and depth of change wrought by the Second Vatican Council is severely limited by the fact that the documents of Vatican II clearly reaffirm the traditional faith and mission of the Church. In order to get around this difficulty, there has arisen an argument that runs as follows:

Actually, Vatican II was only the beginning, the first step in an evolution of the Church that will transform every aspect of the faith and practice of Christians. Therefore, although the decrees of the Council still contain much of the old spirit, this amounts to no more than a necessary concession that the progressive forces had to make in order to secure a majority vote on certain measures. These traditionalistic affirmations should not deceive as to the identity of the underlying trend in the Church and the real spirit of Vatican II—namely, the movement towards modernization in all areas of the life of the Church. And this will mean the modification, transformation and even, perhaps, the abolition of the dogmatic belief of the past.

This thesis could be found two years ago among "advanced" theologians such as Gregory Baum. But today it is even more current. It received a good deal of publicity during the "congress on the theology of Vatican II" held at Toronto last August.

Now, this argument is marked by a curious contradiction: on the one hand, Vatican II is supposed to be accepted by all Catholics as the authoritative voice of the Church (and the "progressives" represent themselves as the champions of Vatican II); on the other hand, the meaning of Vatican II is said to reside wholly in the interpretation of the "advanced" forces in the Church. The Dogmatic Constitution on the Church states that the Fathers of the Council intended their actions to be in strict agreement with the former councils of the Church. But the progressive theologians, professors and journalists assert that the words of the Fathers are not to be taken literally, that the Council represented in reality the beginning of a breaking away from the tradition, the first phase in the modernization of Christian faith itself. Thus, whenever certain laymen, priests and prelates are reminded that a proposal or practice is contrary to the expressed intention of the Council, they reply that the passages quoted are backward looking, inconsistent with the progressive trend of the Council, and should therefore be ignored as unfortunate and embarrassing holdovers from a past that is in the process of being overcome.

But the faithful Christian must ask: Whence do these persons derive the right to place themselves above the Council whenever they find it convenient? Do they believe that they are the only ones who are inspired by the Holy Spirit and can therefore take the liberty of correcting the thinking of the Council? One wonders why the Fathers of the Council did not add a postscript to all of the Council documents in which they confessed that they really did not mean what the words appeared to mean, that there was an esoteric, hidden, secret meaning—the "real meaning" which it is given to a few persons to perceive and communicate to the world; and then the names of these privileged few who are directly inspired by the Holy Spirit could have been listed.

One of the chief devices for discovering the "real meaning" of the Council is to put forward the many unfortunate and dangerous speeches that were made during the course of the Council as representing the key to the correct interpretation of the Council's work—that is, of the "direction in which the Church is moving." Anything that goes contrary to this "direction" or "evolution" (it is assumed) was just a temporary and unimportant accommodation of the "conservatives"; after all, it always takes time to work a fundamental change. But again we must ask: What entitles these persons to interpret the orthodoxy of official documents that affirm the doctrine of the Church as expressed in all former councils as an unessential concession, and to proclaim the progressive ideas found in some speeches of a few prelates the very voice of the Holy Spirit? Should we not rather see the intervention of the Holy Spirit precisely in the fact that these shallow, insipid, quite "advanced" speeches bear no resemblance to the official decrees which reveal the identity of the Church through all the centuries and which possess the flavor of the authentic Catholic spirit?

Where is the guidance of the Holy Spirit to be recognized if not in the protection of the *depositum Catholicae fidei* from all compromise with heresy? Many heretical speeches were delivered in former councils. For example, in the Council of Nicaea it was above all the deacon St. Athanasius who, on the human plane, was responsible for the victory over Arianism; and where can we see the intervention of the Holy Spirit if not in the fact that despite the strong Arian tendencies which were furthered by many members of that council, Arianism was finally condemned? The history of Church councils confirms that it is in the official outcome of a council that we must look for the guidance of the Holy Spirit.

After the Council of Nicaea no faithful Catholic claimed that it was only the first step in a spiritual evolution, the beginning of a trend that would lead to a complete change in the life of the Church. Nor after the First Vatican Council did anyone announce, for example, that the definition of Papal infallibility was "only a beginning," the first of a series of steps that would lead to the abolition of councils of the Church.

One must say simply that those who proclaim that they possess the real meaning of the Council and are able to predict the future have lost their faith in the Church as a divine institution. To them it is a merely natural, human organization and hence subject to the same pressures and influences that may direct the "development" of other purely mundane institutions. Moreover, they have applied to the Church the Hegelian doctrine of evolution in history. For all their arrogant and boastful antipathy to dogma, they have introduced a dogma of their own which they insist that the Catholic world must accept—namely, the evolution of the "World Spirit" in history. If their predictions about the future course of the Church were correct—if it were possible for the faith of the Church to change in accordance with the "climate of opinion" of various epochs, to become "modern" with each new "modern man" that replaces the old one—then the Church would inevitably disintegrate; for a church that could—suddenly or gradually—acquire doctrines that contradicted what she had taught for almost two thousand years would lose her identity and, with it, all legitimate claim to authority.

A church that would be a kind of religious parliament could not possibly interest a truly faithful Christian. And a church subject to a kind of Hegelian evolution (and thereby participating in a general human, historical evolution) has absolutely no place for religious authority. And yet, the progressives want to claim for their church of the future all the authority that they deny to the Church of the past. But the only genuine ecclesiastical authority there can be is that of the Church which remains ever the same in its faith and mission.

Vatican II was a "beginning" only in the sense that every council of the Church has been a beginning: it called for a revivification of souls in the unchanging faith that Christ gave to His Church to safeguard and transmit. It promises not a new Church out of the old, but the same Church ever new.

VIII

The 'Postconciliar Spirit'

The professional *avant-gardistes* in the Church today never tire of telling us of "the Christian faith in the postconciliar epoch"—of the changes called for by the "postconciliar spirit." These vague slogans conceal a tendency to replace the infallible magisterium and unchanging faith of the Church with something else, something "new." I am reminded of the famous program of the German National Socialist Party, which in Paragraph 17 declared that it accepted Christianity insofar as it corresponded to the "Nordic ethos." In that case, too, the divinely-revealed doctrine of the Church was supposed to subordinate itself to an extremely vague and, moreover, *purely natural norm.*

But does not the expression "postconciliar spirit" refer to the "spirit of Vatican II"? And is it not, therefore, something precise and Christian? But even if this were the intended meaning, the effect would be to represent the Second Vatican Council (the "spirit" of its decrees) as an ultimate norm that is played off against the former councils—above all, against the Council of Trent. Now, the moment one implies that one council has rendered others outmoded, irrelevant, the question immediately arises: Whence does one derive the conviction that the truth of the Holy Spirit is to be found more in *this* council than in other ones? In the first place, even if a council could err in its dogmatic definitions, there is no reason to suppose that the latest council is less exposed to error than former ones. But, of course, any contradiction in defined dogma is incompatible with the infallible magisterium of the Church. Any implication, therefore, that Vatican II has in any way abrogated dogmatic expositions of former councils calls into question the divine institution and perpetual guarantee of the Catholic faith.

Furthermore, the Second Vatican Council made no dogmatic definitions; its purpose was strictly pastoral in nature. And Vatican II declared *expressis verbis* the continuity of the "spirit" of its utterances with that of former councils. Thus, one could never legitimately oppose the "spirit of Vatican II" to that of former councils.

The Holy Father gave a clear answer to those who wish to treat Vatican II as a kind of beginning of the authentic Christian revelation, as a new norm against which the teachings of former councils must be measured:

> The teachings of the Council do not constitute a complete, organic system of Catholic doctrine. Doctrine is much more extensive, as everyone knows, and it is not called into question by the Council nor substantively modified. (Address of Pope Paul VI, January 12th, 1966.)

But in all reality the propagators of "the postconciliar spirit" do not truly identify it with the spirit of the decrees of Vatican II. The terms themselves—"postconciliar spirit," "postconciliar Church"—that is, the spirit and the Church *after* the Council, clearly suggest that something quite different is meant. Often this is openly and frankly admitted, as at the Toronto Congress where the Vatican Council was seen by some speakers as only a beginning, but as not fully expressing the "postconciliar spirit." In fact, as we said above, this conveniently vague notion has no basis in the infallible magisterium of the Church. It represents, rather, a mentality nourished by historical relativism and at the service of that fictional creature, "modern man."

Yet, the "postconciliar spirit" cannot justly designate the state of the Church after Vatican II, for no one can deny that there are contradictory currents within the framework of the Church today, not one trend that embraces all Catholics. Thus, it is not even possible to speak of a "postconciliar spirit" that is analogous to the "post-Tridentine mentality." The Council of Trent imposed through its precise and emphatic definitions of faith a lucid unity of spirit on the hierarchy, the clergy, and all of the faithful, a spirit that stamped the time which we know today as the Counter-Reformation.

If we wish to know precisely in what the new modernism that calls itself the "postconciliar spirit" consists, we have only to turn to the numerous warnings of the Holy Father. For example:

> New opinions in exegesis and theology, often borrowed from bold but blind secular philosophies, have in places found a way into the realm of Catholic teaching. Under the pretext of adapting religious thought to the contemporary outlook, they prescind from the guidance of the Church's teaching, give the foundations of theological speculation an historicist direction...and try to introduce a so-called "post-conciliar mentality" among the People of God. (From the Apostolic Exhortation of February 22nd, 1967.)

> [There are] sons of the Church who...seek a Christianity which is noncommittal, non-dogmatic....How can such

weariness of being Catholic derive from the Council? (Address of July 27th, 1966.)

The total unorthodoxy of opposing the Second Vatican Council to past councils could not be more clearly indicated than in the Holy Father's remarks on his Turkish pilgrimage. Speaking of the early councils, he said:

> Thus [they] gave Christianity its basic doctrine, using human thought—as the Apostles had done in the past—to explore the meaning, the theological reality, and to provide religious language with its first unequivocal and irreformable expressions.
>
> This shows the people of our day...how the definitions promulgated by the councils have remained, and must remain, immutable, both in their content and also in the formulas expressing it. (July 30th, 1967.)

If we examine the speeches and writings of the heralds of the "postconciliar spirit," we shall find that the real content of this spirit is the desire to conform to "modern times," to "the scientific age," to "man come of age." (Of course, the new norm is as much a mere specialty of a single epoch as the National-Socialist "ethos of the Nordic race" was a specialty of a single people.)

This "modernization" of the Church is put forward as an attempt to deepen the truth of Christian revelation, to free the deposit of Catholic faith of "mythological elements." But in making the alleged mentality of our epoch the criterion of the Faith, these postconciliar spirits are only replacing the perennial faith with short-lived and often self-contradictory slogans. The fashionable theories that fill the air are usually no more than sophisticated superstitions. In choosing these as the norm for their alleged deepening of the Christian truth, the postconciliarites have in reality set the wolf to mind the sheep.

Perhaps the most pervasive manifestation of the "postconciliar spirit" is the unrestricted freedom many assume in the discussion of religious matters, a penchant for re-examining the dogmas, instead of accepting the deposit of Catholic faith as transmitted infallibly by the Church. But when these postconciliar persons assert that the Church must be adapted to the mentality of our epoch, they have in mind meeting all the objections that are made against the Church—not only by the Protestant denominations, but also by the "world." The deepest desire of some of our progressives seems to be to measure up in the eyes of the world. But this attitude in no way grows out of a genuine thirst for truth, but comes, rather, from an unwarranted respect for the opinions of the world and from fear of the world's censure; it comes from having chosen to replace the infallible magisterium of the Church with certain contemporary opinions.

The absurdity of all of these perversions of the faith is most flagrant in those who assert that they are deepening the truth, after first having proclaimed that there is no "static truth." This self-contradictory position, born out of radical historical relativism, would (if it were possible to take it seriously) make all striving for truth senseless, the appeal to truth an empty gesture, and faith and religion utterly meaningless.

Of course, the unchangeable character of the Church is a scandal to the world and the worldly. But the Catholic should rather affirm this unchangeableness as a sign of her supernatural foundation:

Lo! the fair form of the Ancient Church rises up at once, is fresh and as vigorous as if she had never intermitted her growth. She is the same as she was three centuries ago, ere the present religions of the country existed; you know her to be the same; it is the charge brought against her that she does not change; time and place affect her not, because she has her source where there is neither place nor time, because she comes from the throne of the Illimitable, Eternal God. (John Henry Cardinal Newman, "Prospects Of The Catholic Missioner," in *Discourses to Mixed Congregations*.)

IX

The Corruption of Souls by the New Catechisms

After inspecting some of the new series of grammar-school catechisms, one is led to ask if the authors really believe that theirs is the most efficacious way of communicating to children the true Christian faith. Let us examine the approach of the *Word and Worship* series published by Benziger Brothers. (What is said of this series can also be applied to the catechisms published by Sadlier and by the Paulist Press.)

In the Gospel according to St. Luke we read:

> And a woman named Martha welcomed Him to her house. And she had a sister called Mary, who also seated herself at the Lord's feet, and listened to His word. But Martha was busy about much serving. And she came up and said: "Lord, is it no concern of Thine that my sister has left me to serve alone? Tell her therefore to help me." But the Lord answered and said to her: "Martha, Martha, thou art anxious and troubled about many things; but there is only one thing necessary. Mary has chosen the best part, and it will not be taken from her."

But in the third-grade text, *We Follow Jesus*, Luke 10:30-42 is paraphrased as follows:

> Martha and Mary were close friends of Jesus. Mary was talking to Jesus. Martha came to Jesus. She was worried about cooking the dinner. "Jesus, get Mary to help me," said Martha. But Jesus said: "Now, Martha, do not worry too much about dinner; just do the best you can."

Now, is this blatant falsification of the Gospel—which deliberately omits the very point and essence of the episode—supposed to be some refined pedagogical trick? Jesus' visit to Bethany is made into something so insignificant and pedestrian that there remains no reason whatsoever for including it in the teaching of religion. But the result is worse than an irrelevance: it represents a disfigurement of the sacred humanity of Christ. And this is the general effect of these three new series of catechisms.

It is difficult to believe that a member of the Church in full possession of his faculties would consider such a distortion of the Gospel, of the teaching of Christ, a valid and effective means of transmitting the truth.

What would one say if, for "pedagogical reasons," children were taught that Paul VI was one of the heads of state in the 1960s and was primarily concerned with international affairs, or that William Shakespeare was a sixteenth-century businessman to be remembered for his financial management of a London company, or that Ludwig von Beethoven earned a place in the history of music because he was the father of jazz?

To strip the sacred humanity of Jesus of all features that constitute the epiphany of God, to present Him as a "jolly good fellow" and ordinary person, is to preclude the growth of faith in Christ's divinity.

The *Word and Worship* catechisms pretend to present the message of Christ while omitting all reference to sanctification, to eternal life, to God's judgment, to eternal beatitude, to Hell...while keeping from Catholic students knowledge of the one thing necessary. This is certainly not less of a falsification of Christian revelation and the doctrine of the Church than would be a history of the United States that did not mention the Mayflower Compact, the Declaration of Independence, the Federalist Papers, or the Constitution.

Is it possible for a sincere Christian to believe that the way to draw children to Christ—to the epiphany of God, Him to Whom St. Peter said: "Depart from me, O Lord, for I am a sinful man" (Luke 5:8)—is to tack His Name on to a list of "famous" men in the following way:

> George Washington is famous because he was a great general. Daniel Boone is famous because he was a great Indian scout. Babe Ruth is famous as a great baseball player. Many men are famous for many different reasons. Jesus Christ, however, is famous because he loved people so much.

When Christian saints (those who authentically reflect the sacred humanity of Christ) and even the God-man Himself are placed on the same level as humanitarian philanthropists and controversial political figures like Martin Luther King, the very qualities that distinguish a saint from ordinary men are suppressed and obscured.

Children will never grasp the unique glory of holiness while they are exposed to such an approach. The proper way would be to show them a real moral hero such as Socrates, and then to insist on the radical difference between even such an admirable figure and a Christian saint, a St. Peter, St. John, or St. Francis of Assisi.

But the authors of these books have other concerns. For example, readers of *We Follow Jesus* are told that Paul Tillich was a great Christian. Now, to say the least, he was certainly no Christian—as Professor Freeman of the University of Rhode Island has clearly shown. What can be the authors' point, except to make cruel propaganda for the desacralization of religion? And the interest in "ecumenism" in these books is completely out of place. The classroom is not the place to practice ecumenism, but to present the glorious word of Jesus, the mystery of the Church and the Sacraments, and the heroic lives of the saints. True ecumenism presupposes that Catholics are firmly rooted and educated in the Faith.

The falsification that characterizes *Word and Worship*'s portrayal of Christ in the Gospel is carried over in the presentation of Christian morality and the moral teaching of the Church. The authors consider the teaching of the Ten Commandments an outmoded legalism that has no place in a religion of love. This is in direct contradiction to what Christ taught. He said: "Keep My Commandments." The result of the presentation of Christian morality in these catechisms is that little children are encouraged not to submit to the guidance of the Church, so that they may exercise their "freedom and responsibility."

It is too much to expect one to believe that those who are responsible for these textbooks really intend to convey to the children the authentic doctrine of the Church. We must rather conclude that they intend to spread a new conception of Christianity, one that radically contradicts the doctrine of the Church, the Christian revelation that has been the object of faith for almost two thousand years, from the day of Pentecost to the present. But then, why do these scribblers for false prophets dare to assume the right to teach the Christian religion to Catholic children? Should they not in all honesty cease to present themselves as representatives of the Church introducing children to the Catholic Faith, when they are in fact arbitrarily substituting their secularized Christianity for the genuine doctrine of the Church? Why, if they have lost their faith in the traditional teaching of the Church, will they not stop passing off their own heresies as orthodox doctrine? If they want to remake Christianity into a worldly religion, why don't they at least have the honesty to leave the Church and work at their devilish purpose openly?

They will probably answer that they are not heretics, that they merely wish to present a Christian faith that suits "modern man." But the question remains: Whence do they derive the authority to replace the doctrine of the Church with this "modernized" Christian faith? As soon as they desire to change Christian revelation by adapting it to modern man, as soon as they believe that the mentality of an epoch is the measure of divine revelation, they are no longer Catholics—whether they want to admit this fact or not.

Catholic parents should not be distracted by the evasive argument that all that is at stake is a question of pedagogy and that ordinary Catholics, those who are not specialists in grammar and high school education, are incompetent to criticize this technical educational matter.

One does not have to be a pedagogue to know that the teaching of error is not the best way to lead students to truth. Further, and quite apart from the fact that the authors of these books are not teaching the doctrine of the Holy Catholic Church, the notion that one can lead people to truth by adapting it to their whims and wishes, as if truth were a product for sale or a club seeking members, is completely erroneous. In religion, such an adaptation—even for "pedagogical" purposes—can at most lead to a nominal acceptance of the Christian faith, a faith that has been so adapted, so stripped down, so reduced to a person's peripheral worldly experience that it does not require a conversion for its reception.

Moreover, a child not only does not have hardened convictions that the Christian teacher must overcome, but he has a strong inclination toward religion. One forgets thus that the way to attract the child's soul to God is precisely to present to him the sacred humanity of Christ in its full glory, to confront him with the world above, which surpasses all that this world can offer. This will not be to deprecate natural values, but rather to encourage the child to lift up his heart to something infinitely more beautiful than mere natural values, to glimpse the holiness of Christ's humanity, in Whom only is the natural perfected and sanctified.

The secularizing authors of the new catechisms would have us believe that religion will appear more lively, more vital, to children if it is assimilated to their daily life. But there are many things for which the atmosphere of daily life is asphyxiating rather than invigorating. If we assimilate the notions of good and evil to the familiar experiences of agreeable and disagreeable, successful and unsuccessful, we necessarily falsify the unique nature of these moral categories. Such a reductive approach bars the way to any understanding of the true nature of moral good and evil. For the reality of Christian morality to come alive in the soul, there must be a concentration on the distinction between moral good and evil, moral goodness and sinfulness, and the mundane notions of success and failure, pleasure and displeasure. Only when the true glory of moral good and the unparalleled disgrace of sin are presented in radical distinction to other antitheses, can the soul of the child be vividly and permanently impressed with the meaning of Christian moral teaching.

It is a mere superstition to believe that religion will be made more vivid when assimilated to daily life. As we have seen, assimilation means distortion. If we want to introduce a child to the message of Christ, to permit this mystery to manifest itself in all its unique intensity, then we must begin with the child's highest experiences and ascend by analogy to the new and different message of Christ, always being careful to do justice to its unique solemnity. We should, for example, tell children of the conversions of the great religious personalities and make them acquainted as much as possible with the lives of the saints who are the great proofs of the reality of the redemption of the world through Christ.

It is common for partisans of the new catechisms to justify them by insisting that they represent only necessary "experiments." "Experimentation" will make religion more "lively" to students. For these people, the slogan of "experimentation" conjures pleasant associations of vitality, scientificness, unprejudiced and anti-dogmatic flexibility, promise for the future. For them, any insight not presented as the result of experimentation is considered abstract, unreal, irrelevant. Yet, there are fields in which experimentation is not merely the wrong method and thus unscientific, but indeed totally incompatible with the nature of the subject. So it is with ethics, for example. Experimental ethics is unscientific, self-contradictory, and unethical. The very idea of letting someone commit crimes in order to study ethics is utterly immoral. And to make experiments with the souls of children in order to discover the most efficacious way of teaching religion is an irresponsible disrespect for the children and the very antithesis of a religious attitude. As long as experimentation is confined to mere technical matters—for example, to the problem of developing the memory—there can, of course, be no objections. But when the experimentation affects the content of faith, *as it does in the catechisms we have been discussing*, when it poisons the souls of children with a distorted presentation of Christian revelation, then it becomes a diabolical game, a terrible irreverence against God and innocent children; it becomes a kind of spiritual vivisection, something far worse than medical vivisection on children would be.

But we repeat: Catholic parents should not be distracted by pedagogical arguments. The pedagogy put forward to justify the new catechisms is false. But what we are confronted with here is not a question of pedagogy. Written all over these textbooks which are this very day poisoning the souls of little children is a hatred of the sacred and of the supernatural. This demands more from Catholic parents than arguments: it demands action. The rights of Catholic parents in these matters were reaffirmed by the Second Vatican Council. Their duty in the present hour is clear. They must not tolerate their children's being force-fed a secularized Christianity. They must insist that these texts be removed from the Catholic grammar schools, and they must withhold their children and their financial support from these schools until such vicious books as the *Word and Worship* series are removed.

X

Crisis of Faith or Crisis of Culture?

It has been put forward several times in recent months that the great crisis in the Church today—the spiritual confusion, the unorthodox opinions, the frenetic tampering with Christian tradition—is the product, not of a crisis of faith, but of a "crisis of culture." This thesis is usually followed by the suggestion that what is therefore required of religion today is an adjustment, an "adaptation," to the radical change in culture that is upon us.

But if we consider the contrast between the "new opinions" circulating among many Catholic intellectuals and the doctrine of the Church; if we reflect on the "new theologies" as exemplified by the speculations of the German Jesuit Karl Rahner or the Dominican Eduard Schillebeeckx; if we are aware of the arrogance of Herder & Herder in publishing—in plain defiance of the Vatican—the Dutch catechism in which, for example, the Virgin Birth of Christ and the doctrine of eternal punishment are not mentioned; if we are outraged at the denials of Catholic dogma to be found in a multitude of books and articles written by Catholic priests and laymen, published by the Catholic press, and received enthusiastically in Catholic universities; if we tremble at the injury to

the faith of small children that may be done by such textbooks as the *Word And Worship* series of grammar-school
catechisms in which Christ's personality and teachings are
distorted—if we take note of all or any of these things, we
shall have to conclude that the suggestion that the Church is
faced merely with a "cultural crisis" represents either irresponsible wishful thinking or a diabolical attempt to divert
our attention from the daily growing apostasy.

Moreover, the notion of a "crisis of culture" is itself rather
vague and ambiguous. The term *culture* may properly refer
to many things—from style in art and architecture to habits
of living and fashions of behavior and dress. Thus, we speak
of the cultural features that distinguish the Baroque Age
from the Renaissance, of the difference in culture between
the seventeenth and the eighteenth century, or of the more
radical change in culture that separates the eighteenth from
the nineteenth century. History presents a continual change
in culture. It would be preferable, therefore, not to apply the
term *crisis* to cultural change, but to reserve it rather for the
phenomenon of a decomposition of culture as such, or for
the disappearance of that objectification of the human spirit
which we call *culture*.

But is it not true that we are witnessing a crisis of culture
in the present moment? There certainly is a good deal of
cultural decomposition (for example, the phenomenon
Gabriel Marcel has analyzed in his *Man Against Mass Society*).
But the striking moral decline that characterizes our society,
the growing amoralism, can in no way be described as a
"crisis of culture."

Questions of good and evil, of truth and falsity are essentially beyond culture. What we mean when we speak of
Cain's wickedness, or of Hitler's or Stalin's abominations,
belongs to quite another order than our criticism of bad art.
It is the tactic of those who deny the absolute reality and

validity of the categories of moral good and evil to interpret them as mere cultural phenomena.

It is, of course, true that false philosophies are playing a role in the current crisis of faith. Historical relativism, scientism, evolutionism, materialism, progressivism, and other pseudo-philosophies can be detected in the thinking of some influential Catholics. But those who tell us that these new philosophies reflect the great cultural changes which define modernity and to which the Church must adapt itself not only misrepresent the relationship that has always existed between philosophy and the Church (which can never accept philosophies that deny any of the truths presupposed by Christian revelation); but they also falsify the nature of philosophy.

Any philosophy worthy of the name necessarily claims to be true; it aims at the discovery of truth. The only relevant question one can ask of a philosophy is: Is it true or false? A philosopher's teaching may be basically true but incomplete, or it may be mixed with many errors. It may be fundamentally wrong, but contain true insights. But the difference between a true philosophical thesis and a wrong one is in any case emphatically not a cultural difference.

Cultures do not claim to be "true"; their theme is not truth. One culture may be more or less beautiful than another, more or less refined. Cultures differ in many respects, including general attitudes towards aspects of life. Cultures differ as languages differ. In philosophy, on the contrary, the essential theme is truth.

In all cultures there have been philosophical disputes. One thinks of Socrates and the sophists, of St. Bernard and Peter Abelard, of Descartes and his contemporaries, of Kierkegaard and Hegel. But these and other clashes between truth and error were not manifestations of crises in culture. And the differences between ethical relativism and absolutism, between determinism and indeterminism, between materialism and the recognition of the human spiritual soul cannot be attributed to differences in culture. Although the cultural situation in a given time indeed has an influence on the problems philosophers choose to deal with, the truth of a philosopher's insight is not in the least subject to the changes of culture. A philosophical truth can never be invalidated *by* time, though it can be completed *in* time. Behind the reduction of philosophy to a cultural phenomenon is an attack on the very notion of truth; this is the historical relativism in the name of which modernists have always carried out their attacks on the dogmas of the Church.

The evasion implicit in ascribing the current troubles in the Church to a "cultural crisis" will be further clarified if we consider the relation that obtains between religion and culture. Culture, which is the superabundant, creative objectification of the human spirit, presupposes that the individual and the community stand firm in the truth. Whatever ideas or philosophies men may hold, culture requires for its achievement a reverent contact with being. The decline—indeed, the disappearance—of culture that marks our epoch is not a question merely of an absence of talent, of creative genius. It is primarily a consequence of the loss of the indispensable presupposition of culture—a full and genuine human life; it represents the destructive influence of wrong conceptions of the cosmos, of false philosophies; and, finally, one can see in the disappearance of culture today the decline of true religion which for almost two millennia was the fecundating principle of Western culture.

As one would expect, the most radical of the new modernists and secularizers in the Church do not pretend that the Church is faced with a cultural crisis. They openly assert that the "future of belief" will differ radically from the traditional Catholic creed. They do not hesitate to speak of a crisis of faith—though even that term would be an equivocation in their case. One should rather speak of a loss of faith, of apostasy.

There are three types of Catholics who are obscuring the menace of the intrusion of heresies into the Church by referring to a "crisis of culture."

First, there are those more devious secularizers and self-styled progressives who wish to avoid an open conflict with the guardians of orthodoxy. These persons believe that they can more easily "reform" the Church, transform it into a "modern," a secular institution, by camouflaging their denials of Catholic dogma. This first type is truly diabolical.

Second, there are those who are more interested in their influential positions and material advantages than in matters of faith. There have always been such dignitaries in the Church—more worldly lords than successors of the Apostles. This is an inevitable tribute paid to human frailty. These persons do not have a firmly orthodox faith, nor are they passionate adherents of some heresy, nor are they "reformers." Thus, they cannot be aroused by the spread of heresy. Their main interest is to avoid a fight. They are swimming with what they believe is the trend of the time and they find the slogan of "crisis of culture" a convenient means of explaining away the challenge of heresy so as to avoid difficulties with the Holy See.

The third type is to be found especially among those in authority who refuse to employ authority to stop the spread of heresy. They are afraid of being called "reactionaries" or "ultraconservatives," of being accused of "outdatedness" in the secular press, of losing popularity. So they seek to persuade themselves and the anxious faithful that there is no real danger to faith within the Church today, that orthodoxy is not at stake in the present "cultural crisis." They thus manage to quiet their consciences and avoid their apostolic duty to defend the integrity of the faith; they can avoid the task, for example, of ascertaining whether the utterances of the priests in their dioceses or universities are in agreement with the doctrine of the Church.

But the faithful are not being put off by this evasion. They are following the lead of the Holy Father and, firm in their own faith, are uniting to defend the Church from the secularizers within her.

XI

The Marks of a
True Christian Education

It has become very urgent today to ask what are the marks of a true Christian education. Every faithful Catholic must notice that we are facing a radical destruction of the transmission of Catholic faith in Catholic grammar schools, high schools and colleges. We need only think of the horror of so many new catechisms, such as the Benziger catechism (in which Christ is represented as a mediocre, jolly good fellow), or of the Sadlier and Paulist catechisms, in which the narration of the Gospel is arbitrarily falsified and Christ is, at best, a humanitarian reformer. The Decalogue is dismissed, and an unChristian, so-called "New Morality" replaces it.

Recently, a teacher told me of the way religious instruction is given in a Brooklyn high school staffed by Christian Brothers. Here, the mentioning of God's name is prohibited; everyone who mentions His name is penalized. Psychological studies (moreover of the most doubtful character) are the only topic.

Sometimes teachers of religion are so confused by all the nonsense propagated by famous theologians, that they no longer know if they may present as absolute truth the teaching of the Church about God, Christ, the sacraments and the Church herself. They believe they have to present these doctrines as things not absolutely true. They believe they must stress to their pupils that today many dogmas of the deposit of Catholic Faith are questioned and thus are subject to revision or denial in the future.

Any person with such convictions is no longer entitled to teach religion. By his doubting attitude he clearly proves that he can no longer sincerely call himself a Catholic. He is definitely dishonest if he presents himself to the children or to their parents, or to anyone, as a Catholic and then goes on to implant the illusion that his subjective ideas or the ideas of some fashionable theologians are Catholic doctrine.

Such a teacher disseminates doubt instead of faith. He does the opposite of what the Church and the parents of the children expect him to do. He cheats both the Church and the parents who have confided their children to him. These unfortunate teachers are so naive that they allow their faith to be shaken by the mere fact that some incompetent theologians deny the absolute truth of the dogmas. They uncritically accept as absolute truth the dogmas of the false prophets and the heretical professors of theology. But what the Church has taught for 2000 years is suddenly uncertain!

The Church's Teaching Must Be Unconditionally Accepted

In truth, only that person has the right to teach religion in the frame of the Catholic Church who accepts unconditionally the Creed of Nicaea—as well as the Creed of Pope Paul VI; the dogmas, the official teaching of the Church about morals; and the infallibility of the Pope as defined in Vatican Council I and reaffirmed in Vatican Council II.

It is a grave error, solemnly condemned by Pius VI 200 years ago, to claim that the seat of infallibility could be shifted from the Pope to a "consensus of all the faithful." The mind of the majority can never be an argument for the truth of revelation, any more than it can be for any natural truth. The authority of the Pope has its roots in the institution of Peter by Christ. As Pius VI says:

> That proposition is heretical which states that power has been given by God to the Church that it might be communicated to the pastors who are its ministers for the salvation of souls, if it is thus understood to mean that the power of ecclesiastical ministry and rule is derived from the community of the faithful and given to the pastor. In addition, the proposition is heretical which states that the Roman Pontiff does not receive from Christ in the blessed Peter, but from the Church, the power of ministry which as successor of Peter, true Vicar of Christ and head of the whole Church, he possesses in the universal Church.

Neither would the consensus of all bishops possess infallibility unless it occurred in an official council and in full concert with the Pope. There have been enough heretical bishops in the history of the Church; indeed, in the fourth and fifth centuries the majority of bishops adhered to the heresy of Arius.

In this context we must also especially warn against another dangerous slogan: "the message of the Gospel." Today, many who oppose some teaching of the official magisterium defend themselves by saying that they believe only in the message of the Gospel. If this means that they deny any other religious authority but the Gospel, that they deny the holy tradition of the Church and her being guided by the Holy

Spirit, it would be a mere repetition of Luther's theory. This doctrine of Luther has been refuted by many great theologians and solemnly condemned in the Council of Trent. It is impossible to detach the four Gospels from the living tradition of the Church: Pentecost and the teaching of the Apostles preceded the writing of the four Gospels. Luther also claimed that every individual reader of the Gospel would be enlightened by the Holy Spirit in grasping the authentic content. But the innumerable sects in the frame of Protestantism clearly testify that this assumption of Luther was an illusion, and that the Gospels need an authoritative interpretation.

But today the reduction of Christ's revelation to the message of the Gospel assumes still a very different character than in Luther. Luther's reduction was an error, but at least he believed absolutely in the divine inspiration of every word in the Gospel. But today the appeal to the "message of the Gospel" is a pure slogan, because the same people who transfer all authority exclusively to the Gospel "demythologize" the Gospel, deny its divine inspiration, and make the authentic content of the Gospel dependent upon the allegedly scientific work of exegetes. This Luther would never have tolerated. It is a grotesque idea to make our faith in God and Christ, in the life, deeds, miracles and words of Christ and in His revelation, dependent upon so-called scientific research which has proclaimed more than one hundred different theories in the course of the past 150 years.

Who Decides Which is the True Message?

Moreover, we are confronted here with many different versions of the message of the Gospel. Who is to decide which is its true message? No, we have here but an empty slogan, which is substituted for the teaching of the Church.

Certainly, we do not claim that religious education was perfect prior to the outbreak of the crisis in the Church. There were no doubt many shortcomings. Thus Vatican Council II was eager to improve religious education, to make it more impressive, to vivify it, to attract souls to Christ through it. But the former shortcomings were incomparably less grave than the dissolution and falsification of dogma which we find today. The former shortcomings were marked by insufficiency; the present ones have a destructive character.

Truth and Error Are Incompatible

First, it does not suffice to present the true position on any matter: one must also refute the errors which in a special epoch are, so to speak, in the air and which threaten to infiltrate the Church and confuse the faithful. Truth cannot be fully elaborated without distinguishing it from similar-sounding errors. The glorious history of the Church shows us how the more explicit elaboration of the revelation of Christ went hand in hand with the refutation and condemnation of heresies. Thus, in the refutation of Arianism, the divinity of Christ and the mystery of the Holy Trinity were clearly and explicitly inserted into the Creed.

Second, many people do not grasp the incompatibility of error and truth, when heresies are presented to them with similar words and in a religious tone. Many people, for example, who are quite orthodox and who want to be faithful to the teaching of the Church, admire Teilhard de Chardin. They are not aware of the absolute incompatibility between Christian revelation and his application of evolution to the spiritual nature of man, his interpretation of sin as a mere lower stage of evolution, or his denial of Original Sin and the dogmas of the Church about Original Sin and redemption.

They do not grasp that the "Christ Omega," the principle or force determining evolution, is incompatible with the Jesus Christ of the Gospel, the God-man and Redeemer.

The general danger of overlooking the incompatibility of error and truth is further increased today when there is a question of wrong religious theories, that is to say, heresies. Irenicism makes many believe that calling heresies by their right name is somehow uncharitable. This irenicism is a misinterpretation of the beautiful ecumenical spirit of Vatican Council II, which is eager to see all the positive elements in other religions and which is especially eager to do justice to the genuine Christian faith of many orthodox Protestants—without in any way blurring what divides the authentic Catholic faith from them, and without ever making any compromises.

But our attitude toward a real lover of Christ, a Billy Graham, for instance, may not be extended to Catholics who spread heretical ideas, such as the many alleged "famous theologians" and "progressive" Catholic laymen. First of all, Billy Graham does not claim to present the deposit of Catholic faith; thus we can joyfully acknowledge that, notwithstanding his separation from our Church, he has a great love for Christ, and a firm unshakable faith in many fundamental elements of Christian revelation. Second, he fights within the frame of Protestantism precisely the same fashionable heresies of liberalism, secularism and naturalism which afflict the orthodox Catholic Church.

False Prophets Within the Church Are Not Catholics

The false prophets within the Catholic Church, on the other hand, first of all claim to be the authentic Catholics and thus they fight the alleged conservatives; second they deny, not only those Catholic dogmas which Graham himself does not accept, but also the most elementary truths which we share with Graham. They rather are adherents of the liberalism, secularism and naturalism which Graham fights in Robinson, Cox and Fletcher. And so the very ecumenical attitude which moves us to walk together with Graham a good part of the way moves us also to fly from the company of the heretical and apostate Catholics. Apart from irenicism, which has been explicitly denounced in its falsehood in Vatican Council II, a most unfortunate slogan is gaining wide acceptance: "We must be positive and take a positive approach to all novelties." This slogan seduces many into overlooking the incompatibility of the present grave heresies with the doctrine of the Church. This slogan of "the positive approach" has a magic influence on many. In truth, however, it conceals many grave confusions. There is no attitude toward any object that, in itself, is positive. The "no" spoken to error is as positive as the "yes" spoken to truth. It is only the reverse side of the yes to truth. It implies the same objectivity, the same love for truth, the same reverence before reality, the same transcendence.

Whether we should say yes or no depends exclusively on the nature of the object. To say "no" to truth and "yes" to error is the real negative attitude. The truly positive answer is the one that is dictated by the nature of the object. It is the same in the field of truth as in the moral field. To say "no" to a disvalue is as positive as to say "yes" to a value. Thus the claim to take a positive attitude toward errors, especially when divine revelation is at stake, is nonsensical. This allegedly positive attitude is in reality a most negative one.

Moreover, those false prophets who insist on a positive approach to their destructive heresies are aggressively "negative" when the established doctrines of the Church are in question, or when the declarations of the Holy Father are at stake, e.g. the encyclical *Humanae Vitae*. Thus, the inventors of this slogan do not even take it seriously themselves as soon as they disagree with someone else's position. Still there is no doubt that this slogan confuses many people; it hinders them from recognizing the incompatibility of the doctrines of the false prophets with the authentic Catholic faith to which they still want to adhere.

Errors Must Be Refuted

If, therefore, we want to expound the true marks of religious education it is indispensable that we include the unmasking of the present errors filling the air. We must refute the slogans which confuse many faithful and pious people because they fail to grasp their heretical character and their incompatibility with the true Christian Faith. Four basic errors concerning religious education are now making headway in the alleged "reform" of religious teaching. Let us briefly examine each one of them.

The first error is the myth of "modern man"; it proclaims the total change of man's nature in our times. Man is alleged to have changed so radically that we can no longer expect him to have the same approach to faith and to the Church as in the past 2000 years. Because man now lives in the industrialized world, he has allegedly undergone a complete change; he can more and more dominate the world through progress in technology. And this supposedly makes him a different creature.

This myth of "modern man" has been invented by some sociologists but, unfortunately, it has been accepted by many as the simple and indubitable truth. Certainly, exterior life has changed very much, but man himself has not changed. The sources of his happiness are the same as they ever were: love, marriage, family, friendship, beauty, truth and, above all, peace of soul—a good conscience. His moral dangers are the same as ever before: pride and concupiscence and their fruits, evil passions, ambition, envy, lust of power, avarice, covetousness and so on. The same can be said of the moral virtues he is called upon to realize: justice, honesty, purity, generosity, humility and charity. Today he has the same fate as he had before, the same capacities of mind, knowledge and free will; the same heart, which can rejoice and suffer; the same destiny. He is as much in need of redemption as before. To him the words of St. Augustine apply today as much as before: "Thou hast made us for Thyself, O Lord, and our hearts are restless until they rest in Thee."

From what source indeed do the sociologists know that man today has totally changed? On what do they base the existence of this "modern man"? Have they perhaps taken a poll and asked every man whether he is such a "modern man," with completely different needs, for whom the same moral norms no longer apply? Certainly not. And how can those who proclaim in the same breath that all knowledge is timebound in its validity assume that their thesis of the "modern man" will not be the object of laughter in fifty years?

Man's Nature Does Not Change

In reality, man's nature does not change in history. You need only read Plato's dialogues or Herodotus to see that man remains always the same in his basic structure. There is but one radical change in history: the Advent of Christ, the Redemption of man through His death on the Cross, the gift of the life of grace through Baptism. Thus, by his vocation to holiness each man is called upon to permit this change in himself.

Notwithstanding the identity of man's nature through all epochs of history, of course there are still great differences between men in their mentality and in their moral and intellectual standards. But these differences are to be found among men of any epoch. The claim of the complete change in man is, therefore, a myth, not only because man's nature has not basically changed, but also because modern man is a myth, as if in one epoch men have all the same mentality and structure! This is a completely arbitrary claim without any scientific foundation. As a matter of fact, the difference of mentality is still greater between men in one and the same epoch than is the contrast between the different epochs themselves.

A Fatal Influence

This myth of the "modern man" has a fatal influence on education—especially religious education. Too many religious pedagogues believe that a child today must get a completely different religious nourishment. They take it for granted that the religious education of former times can no longer be fruitful today, not because it had shortcomings, but because it was addressed to a youth who no longer exists today. They take it for granted that they must adapt methods of teaching, and even the content of the teaching, to this mythical being, the modern man. They fail to recognize the basic sameness of man's nature in all times—including the sameness of youth. Man has always the same spiritual needs, the same dangers, such as self-deception, the same immaturity during the age of puberty, the same temptations of the flesh, the same ultimate thirst for God of the *anima naturalitatis Christiana*—of the soul "naturally Christian." Man's nature is always susceptible to the same revolt against authority on the one hand and to the same fascination with fake "teachers" on the other. Man has always the same need and thirst in the depth of his soul for guidance by a true authority. Instead of seeing all this, these pedagogues fall prey to the illusory concept of a "modern youth" which can allegedly be reached only through a completely new type of religious education. But the worst effect of this myth is that these pedagogues believe that not only the methods must be changed but also the *content* of religious education. That is to say: religious truth itself must be adapted to this modern mind. Such an attitude obviously leads to the inanity of wanting to modify the divine revelation entrusted to the magisterium of the Holy Church and to adapt it to the alleged spirit of an epoch: a contradiction in itself.

The Second Error

The second basic error is the belief that *experimentation* must be introduced in religious education in order to find out the most efficient way of leading the souls of the young people to an unconventional but vital religious life. At the basis of this notion of experimentation is the fetishization of natural science—the naive belief that the only method of attaining any certainty in knowledge is that of the laboratory and thus, of the "experimental approach."

One forgets that this can lead to results only in certain areas and that its use in other areas is the peak of unscientific method. It is nonsensical (and quite impossible) to use the experimental approach in such spiritual areas as morality, religion, marriage and love, and in such intelligible topics as logic, epistemology, metaphysics, aesthetics and ethics. With respect to all these subjects we can attain results only through a completely different method. These are all cases in which an intuitive insight—a true evidence—can and must be attained. Experiments here are nonsensical. No one would say: We must make experiments in order to know that two plus two is four or to discover the law of contradiction.

But experimentation in some of these realms cannot be ruled out of question simply because it is inane, inapplicable and sterile—that is, for epistemological reasons; in some cases it must be ruled out because it is also immoral; incompatible with the reverence certain things demand, or with the very nature of a being. Experimentation implies the possibility of a control and repetition of a happening under the same circumstances. Now there are many realms where the same circumstances cannot be produced in successive attempts and where the testing of something is, moreover, contradictory to the very nature of something. Suppose a man says: Let us make experiments about contrition; you must first commit theft and then adultery and then we shall observe whether your contrition has the same character in both cases. The absurdity and immorality of such a proposal should be obvious to anyone who has kept his sanity. Not only does the seriousness of any sin forbid such experimental research but, moreover, it is impossible to make sinning an object of experimentation. Neither observation by another person, nor self-observation, can lead to any valuable result because true contrition is focused on God and on our having offended Him. As soon as I make of it an "experiment" by looking at it in a neutral laboratory attitude, it is no longer contrition.

Such a horrible and inane type of experimentation is but a fake performance, of the sort to be found in the awkward book of Masters and Johnson, where sexual intercourse is made an object of laboratory studies.

We all know with what enthusiasm experimentation is advocated by many in the fields of liturgy and of religious education. They believe that in order to overcome conventionalism in education—which was undoubtedly widespread in the recent past—experimentation is the remedy. Experimentation is hailed as a realistic method; it puts us in living contact with reality, it replaces theories with facts and it allows us to hearken to reality in its plenitude and variety. But this very belief that experimentation is the only way to a living contact with reality is, in truth, itself a pure abstract theory—and an erroneous one at that! It makes a mere laboratory out of life and the plenitude of being, with all its flavor, beauty and richness.

In order to know what is the best method of religious education, we must certainly hearken to reality. But this hearkening is opposed not only to abstract theories but just as much to experimentation. Hearkening to reality here means a deep analysis on the one side, of the nature of religion, and on the other, of the adequate way to transmit religious truth to souls. This latter task demands an analysis of the human soul in general, and of the nature of each youngster in particular. What is essential here is a reverent attitude, a wondering, which is the basis of true philosophy. Given this attitude and also the desire to grasp the intelligible elements of being in their real nature, we can hope to attain a deeper understanding of the true marks of religious education, and to discover the causes of former shortcomings. Such truths disclose themselves only to this reverent, cooperating attitude and never to the neutral laboratory approach.

It is simply immoral to make of the souls of children an object of experimentation with regard to the one thing necessary, to the all-important question of faith and union with Christ. This approach undermines *ab ovo* any true religious education; it is a kind of spiritual vivisection, an abomination in the eyes of God.

The Third Error

The third basic error is the wrong conception of vivification. The new pedagogues say that religion should not remain something abstract for the youngster, something separated from his daily life, something of which he thinks in church but quickly forgets after he leaves church; something so alien, so far up in the clouds that he can never be at home with it, never feel familiar with it.

Thus, continue these pseudo-reformers, we must present religion in a way that fits well into the daily life of the youngster, that becomes a part of the world in which he normally moves and lives. We must adapt religion in its content to the present time; we must tailor it to the mentality of our epoch so that the youngster can easily accept it. Religious lessons must be combined with things that amuse and attract him.

So too, they go on, must worship be adapted. The Mass should be interspersed with jazz and rock-and-roll so that the youngster feels at home. He will then see religious worship not as a mere boring duty but as something joyful and alive. This conception of a "living religion" betrays a complete ignorance of the nature of religion and of Christian revelation. It entails not the vivification, but the burial of religion. The true vivification of religion consists in the very opposite of what the progressives think.

No doubt, the evil of a mere "conventional" religion was widespread in the last 50 years before Vatican Council II. By conventional religion I mean one where the relation of a man to Christ and His Holy Church is considered by him as a mere loyalty, similar to the loyalty he has for the State whose citizen he is. He is a Catholic because he was born a Catholic; and he belongs to the Church just as he belongs to his family and to his country. He fulfills the obligations issuing from this fact as a matter of course; so he goes to church on Sunday and at least once a year he goes to confession and Communion. He marries in the Church and does not remarry if he is unfortunate enough to be divorced, and so on.

Religion is thus considered as a normal part of this conventional man's life—it belongs to his life. And he has not the slightest desire to question the religion into which he was born. But he never accomplishes any real confrontation with Christ. Never once does he realize man's need for redemption; never does he grasp the fact that Christ has redeemed us. He never senses the absolute, new, and sacred world of God. He has no spiritual eyes for the supernatural reality which is revealed to us in the sacred humanity of Christ. This conventional religious man has never wondered about the miracle of the very existence of the Church, about the fact that she has given birth to innumerable saints, each of them being a univocal proof of the redemption of the world by Christ. He has never seen in a saint a luminous example of the very goal of our life, the very *raison d'être* of our existence: To glorify God through our being transformed in Christ, to become a new creature in Christ.

As soon as we have understood the true nature of a living, existential religion which is the real antithesis to a mere conventional religion, we easily see that the attempt to blur the difference between the natural and supernatural is precisely the way to conventionalize religion and to undermine the possibility of a truly lived Christianity. The shortcomings of the past were rooted precisely in the fact that religious truths were presented in an abstract, conceptual way. The awesome reality of the supernatural, and its complete difference from the natural, were never elaborated upon in the correct style and manner—namely, one that would afford the student an intuitive living awareness of the great things before him. Faith, then, became conventional because no one sufficiently prepared the soul of the youngster for a grasping of the infinite beauty and glory of Christ's revelation; no one sufficiently developed his sense for the sacred, for the intrinsic beauty of holiness, for perceiving the abyss that separates holiness from efficiency; no one sufficiently disclosed to him the difference between any earthly happiness and the ultimate happiness which Jesus alone can pour into the soul of every one who believes in Him and loves Him—a happiness which can be present and savored already in this earthly life.

A Bitter Irony

And what a bitter irony we now face! Whereas personal contact with the sacred was formerly omitted by a kind of bureaucratic sleepiness, it is now systematically prevented by the alleged progressive who blurs the difference between sacred and profane, and suppresses the sense of the supernatural. And this is done in the name of deconventionalizing faith and making it living. It is a peculiar cure which aims to fight a disease by producing more of the very disease. Nor is this a case of immunizing by inoculation. The "cure" of secularism is prescribed by those pedagogues who have lost the true faith. They no longer understand the radically different levels in man's soul; the one to which God appeals and where man is attracted to God, and the one to which worldly pleasures appeal, the spirit of the world. They are satisfied if the young people are attracted to religious teaching. They never ask just why the young are attracted: Is it because of the authentic word of Christ? Or is it that what is offered to them has been adapted so much to the atmosphere and spirit surrounding them in a desacralized and dehumanized world—which for all that has an attractiveness of its own—that the content of religion is completely falsified?

The Fourth Error

And this brings me to the fourth error. In their eagerness to make religious teaching more successful, the new pedagogues forget the nature of real success, which alone is at stake here. They are satisfied if a means is successful, even if this success is completely antithetical to the real goal. They undermine the real meaning and *raison d'être* of religious education, which is exclusively to transmit to the young people the untarnished teaching of the Church, to plant in their souls a deep, living, unshakable faith, and to stir in them a love for Christ, a thorough desire to follow Christ and to live according to God's commandments.

These pedagogues congratulate themselves on the brilliant success of their "new approach" to religious teaching; it never seems to dawn on them that the attractiveness of their method was purchased by their repudiating the very truths and supernatural realities which they supposedly aimed at imparting. Their "success," then, is comparable to that of the surgeon who boasts: "The operation was a brilliant success—but the patient died." The end at which they aim and which gives the operation its meaning is sacrificed for the sake of the brilliancy of the operation.

The faith of any young people who have undergone this unfortunate treatment is no longer the true Christian Faith. A secularized humanitarian creed which lacks all the basic features of Christ's revelation has been inculcated in their minds.

They no longer believe in Original Sin, the need of redemption, the fact of our having been redeemed by Christ's death on the Cross. They no longer believe in the one thing necessary, our transformation in Christ, our personal loving relation to Christ. They are completely ignorant of the true charity that can arise exclusively in the heart that loves God above all—God as He has revealed Himself in Christ. Knowledge of what faith they have does not include the role of contrition, the horror of sin, the glorious supernatural union of all members of the Mystical Body of Christ.

Just what sense or meaning has a religious teaching, what *right* has it to exist, if it leads to a creed which has more affinity with the *New York Times* than with the Gospel and the deposit of faith? What does it matter if many young people are attracted to this pseudo-religious teaching? Why is it people are attracted to this pseudo-religious teaching? Why is it noteworthy if this pseudo-Catholicism is accepted easily and joyfully by the youth, if they "cooperate" with the teacher without difficulty? Truly this success is a fake success. It perhaps affords a satisfaction for the teacher's vanity, but it is the burial of true faith and the betrayal of the teacher's true vocation. This teaching operation is indeed "successful." The faith of the students is dead!

The true antithesis to a conventional Christianity is the aliveness rooted in the authentic Catholic Faith, the unshakable faith in the *Credo* that our Holy Father Pope Paul VI solemnly proclaimed at the end of the Year of Faith. It is the deep love for Christ, the will to follow Him, the longing for Christ, the love for His Church, the grasping of her beauty and splendor, the profound gratitude to God for all His gifts.

If we understand the above, we can more clearly elaborate the marks of true religious education and the requisites for a really successful religious education. First, the content of our faith must not be presented as a mere topic of learning, such as history or mathematics. It must be presented in its absolute uniqueness, in the spirit of the Mass of Easter Saturday: *Annuntio vobis gaudium magnum*—I announce to you a great message of joy. The fundamental truths must be presented to the young hearers in such a manner that the ineffably holy atmosphere of revelation is conveyed to them. A supernatural aura must surround these truths: the creation of the world and of man, the fall of Adam, Original Sin, the revelation of the Old Covenant, God speaking to Abraham and to Moses, the tremendous revelation of the Decalogue and the solemn, overwhelming voice of all the prophets, especially Jeremiah and Isaiah; and then the ineffable mystery of the Incarnation, the epiphany of God in Christ, the self-revelation of God in the sacred humanity of Christ, the miracles of Christ, the eternal words of Christ, His death on the Cross, His glorious Resurrection and Ascension, and Pentecost, the birth of the Holy Church.

All this requires the deep faith of the teacher himself. We can never overrate the importance of the irradiation of the personality of the teacher, his own reverent approach to these mysteries, and the avoiding of any atmosphere of sloppiness, self-indulgence and slang in his style. Not only must he be deeply rooted in the Christian Faith—in his love of and faithfulness to the Church—he must also emanate this in his way of teaching, in his dialogue with the students. His deep sense for the supernatural and his love for Christ must pervade his teaching. And in this moment the student must not be a schoolboy for him, a mere pupil as in other lessons, but rather a soul loved infinitely by Christ.

The truly successful teacher of religion must also avoid a fault which has often been committed in the past, the abuse of authority. Hard, pedantic, bureaucratic authority imposed on children and young people is as such something unfortunate, but especially in the context of religious education. We must emphatically stress, however, that a complete absence of authority is still much worse—a weak yielding to the whims of the young people or a smug familiarity, a tone of comradeship, a tone—the French expression—of *frère et cochon*.

Approaching the youngster in a recollected manner, in which a noble reserve is interwoven with a great love, the teacher should act as a real authority. He must also try to show the young people the beauty and dignity of true authority and its difference from the pseudo-authority which so easily gains power over youth. I mean the pseudo-authority of those who are able to impress youth by their slogans, by their alleged independence, and by presenting themselves as the pioneers of the future, as the modern, fashionable oracles. It is a great and important task, especially today, to make young people skeptical towards these fashionable but false prophets. These prophets must be unmasked and recognized for the shallow men that they are. Their mostly self-contradictory theories must be exposed. And they themselves must be stigmatized in their character as ephemerae.

Freedom or Slavery

The teacher cannot show enough that being fascinated by the pseudo-authority of modern false prophets is the greatest intellectual slavery, and an abdication of one's freedom of mind. But to submit to the sacred authority of God and His Holy Church makes us, on the contrary, free. It gives us the possibility to see everything in its true light, to discover the true hierarchy of goods, to be freed from gregarious instincts and above all from enslavement by our own pride.

In this context a great shortcoming of past religious education must be mentioned: one that failed to show the beauty and depth of high natural goods, such as human love, friendship, marriage, and beauty in nature and art. This was a great mistake. When the teacher awakens the sense for high human goods, and shows the difference between these and merely amusing goods or worldly goods such as fame, money and exterior success, he prepares the souls of his pupils for the ascension to the incomparably higher supernatural goods. These high natural goods are a reflection of God's infinite glory, a high gift from His bounty. They are able to evoke the nostalgia for the Absolute, Whom they reflect in a natural way. St. Augustine stresses this admirably in his *Confessions.*

Certainly, all created goods can also distract us from God if we get too attached to them, if we idolize them. But on the other hand, they also have this great positive mission: to draw our minds upward and to prepare our souls for the supernatural message of God. And when we have found Christ, when our hearts are touched by the supernatural good, when we grasp the incomparable superiority of the supernatural over all the natural, then the true natural goods are not discarded. Rather, they are transfigured by Christ and we are even able to see more deeply into their value. "In the light, we see light," says the psalmist.

One of the most urgent tasks of religious education today is to develop the moral sense of the pupils, to evoke in their souls the sense for the breathtaking beauty and splendor of moral values and a deep horror for sin.

Amoralism is today one of the most catastrophic symptoms of spiritual decay and a special threat for the true relation to Christ. And here again we must say that the world of morality has often been presented in a too abstract and too negative way. Statements about the goodness or badness of an act, moreover, have been based upon weak arguments. This should be corrected.

The ultimate seriousness of the categories of moral good and evil must be exposed. One should insist on the primacy of moral values with respect to all other values. Moral values alone have an eternal resonance. Already Socrates saw this primacy when he said: "It is better for man to suffer injustice than to commit it."

But one must also immunize the young people against the unfortunate New Morality, which is neither new nor moral. It is nothing but an exhuming of the mediocre bourgeois utilitarianism of Jeremiah Bentham. And like Bentham's ethics, it misses the very existence of moral values; it is focused only on extra-moral goods.

The Beauty of Purity and Other Virtues

We often hear today that in the recent past the sixth commandment has been over-stressed. This is certainly correct. But the fault consisted not in stressing the importance of purity but in not stressing enough the other moral virtues, such as humility, generosity, liberality and charity. The progressive Catholic today falls prey to the terrible error which, instead of emphasizing all the Christian virtues, becomes blind alike to the grave sin of impurity and to the deep nobility and beauty of purity.

The past mistake consisted not in overrating the importance of purity, but in neglecting the others. It was the fault of one-sidedness. The present blindness to purity is really a case of alleged improvement to which the words of the Gospel apply: "The last state of the man becomes worse than the first."

Granted that purity was presented in an inadequate way to the young people in the past and that the sinfulness of impurity was supported by weak arguments, which, moreover, stressed only the negative; the urgent task today is to present both the beauty of purity and the sinfulness of impurity with better arguments, and to show that all impurity is a desecration of the high destiny of sex—which is to serve as the mutual irrevocable self-donation in the sacrament of marriage. What must be taught is not the neutral, scientific aspect of sex—which is offered today in alleged Catholic schools as sex education, and which verges often on pornography—but the mystery of sex, the relation of this sphere to spousal love, to the desire of the lover to reach an ultimate union with the beloved in this deep mutual self-donation.

The Christian View of Sex

Sex is not a mere instinct, not a mere biological reality. Any approach to sex dictated by the norms of the natural sciences is fundamentally incapable of understanding the true nature of sex. Sex is something which, in its human aspect, can be understood only in its relation to spousal love. It must be approached with deep reverence; it must also be the teacher's aim to evoke reverence in the souls of the young people confronted with the mystery of sex. The wrong alternatives must disappear: either sex is taboo, or it is a neutral affair which can be discussed with an attitude proper to laboratories. No, human sex is a great mystery, something deeply intimate. The teacher's aim must be to show, with great discretion, the beauty of this mystery when actualized according to its God-given meaning. Simultaneously he must show the horror, the gravity, of the sin of impurity.

The Key to Understanding Sex

Spousal love is the key to the true understanding of sex. And, to repeat, sex can be understood only in its destination to serve as a mutual, irrevocable self-donation to the beloved in marriage, and to constitute the ultimate union of marriage. It is against this background that the great mystery must be shown, namely, that God has confided to this union of love the engendering of a new human being. Human sex thus cooperates with the creative act of God.

A Grave Responsibility

Great is the responsibility of the religious educator in the present moment. In the midst of the waves of apostasy among Catholics, in the midst of the deplorable disintegration taking place in the Church, it is a difficult but a glorious task to swim against the stream and to help establish in the souls of the young a firm and unshakable Catholic faith. It is a glorious task to awaken in the young the true love for Christ, the longing for an always greater union with Him, the firm will to follow God's commandments, and the resolve to approach all the great natural goods in the light of Christ and with deep gratitude to God. To fulfill this task rightly, a religious educator will have to face many persecutions coming not only from the world, but also and especially from false brothers. But such persecutions should never frighten him into making compromises. The words of Our Lord should always be before the teacher's mind: "Whoever causes one of the little ones who believe in Me to sin, it were better for him to have a great millstone around his neck and to be drowned in the deepest sea."

These words assume today a special impact because of the horror of present sex education and of the "new morality." But they also apply to every great harm done to the immortal souls of the young by the teachers of false doctrines. In fact, the worst harm that can be inflicted on a soul is to cause it to lose faith in the revelation of Christ and the infallible teaching of His Church.

As in all difficult tasks, however, we are able to take great consolation in the words of St. Paul that *nothing can separate us from the love of Christ*. Let the faithful teachers of religion approach their great and noble task full of hope and fervent ardor. Let them keep in mind that Our Lord has said:

"Heaven and earth shall pass away, but My words shall not pass away."

XII

Academic Freedom and
the Catholic University

Slogans often appear to possess an unassailable validity, to eliminate all possible further consideration, analysis or questioning. This characteristic proceeds from a thoroughly unscientific charlatanry whereby strong emotions are evoked so as to overrun the intellect. Effective slogans are expressions that touch the heart of the hearer by reason of the nobility of their original meaning. Once they are made into slogans, however, these expressions are applied to things that they do not fit. Under the cover of a noble connotation, therefore, ideas are propagated that are not only different but also even antithetical to the original meaning of the expression.

Freedom is such a term; it rightly evokes in man the impression of something noble and of high value. But the slogans "freedom of speech" or "academic freedom" borrow the character of an absolute, which they definitely do not possess, from the absoluteness of moral freedom. They are then often applied to situations in which they function as weapons to abolish freedom.

The Differing Types of Freedom

Before we analyze in detail the exact nature of these special freedoms, we must first briefly hint at the different basic types of freedom. There is first the great gift which God has given man, the ontological freedom of will. Man alone is a *person*, in contradistinction to all other earthly creatures, and thus he alone is not simply ruled by a necessitating causality. Rather, he can freely take positions, he can say yes or no to an invitation to act in a certain way.

This freedom of will is the basis of all responsibility and it is necessarily presupposed in any being that is capable of bearing moral values and disvalues. The decisive importance of this freedom need not be insisted upon here. As St. Augustine marvelously shows, however, there is still another freedom, namely, moral freedom. We are morally free only when we conform to that which is objectively right—to the call of values, ultimately to the commandments of God.

This moral freedom presupposes ontological freedom, but it also implies that we are not enslaved by our pride and concupiscence. Our ontological freedom is abused as long as we follow only the invitations of our pride and concupiscence. Ontological freedom tends in its very meaning and value to moral freedom, in which we follow the commandments of God and freely choose what pleases God. Every person possesses ontological freedom as long as he is not mentally ill. It is a capacity bestowed on man, like reason. We do not give it to ourselves. Moral freedom, on the contrary—that is, the right use of ontological freedom —, is something which depends on us, something for which we are responsible. Here, therefore, the words of St. Augustine apply: "He who made thee without thee will not justify thee without thee."

Unfortunately, however, for many persons today, freedom means the total absence of limits on their actions. To be free means, for these persons, to be unhindered in following their whims and desires. This alleged freedom, in which we refuse to admit any bounds or limitations to our subjective desires, is not only the opposite of moral freedom and responsibility, but also a complete illusion. The truth, whether we like it or not, is that we are all surrounded by many limitations of this arbitrary freedom.

The Limitations on Freedom

The simple fact is that man lives, not as a Robinson Crusoe, but as a member of different communities which impose all kinds of limitations on this arbitrary freedom. His rights confront the rights of other persons and of the communities in which he lives. The good of his individual neighbor and the common good of his society impose many obligations on him which limit his arbitrary freedom. Let us not forget, also, that even in all those cases in which no other human person or community has a right to hinder us from following our likings, our arbitrary freedom is still subject to all the moral commandments and to God.

We turn now to those types of freedom which make the headlines today, for instance, freedom of speech. This refers to the right to say what we think, to utter our conviction. Now it is not difficult to see that this right is a very relative one. Certainly there are cases in which we have not only the right, but also the duty, to speak up. Thus, we should protest and raise our voices against the spreading of evil errors and of immorality. Today, for instance, we have the duty to speak against the horror of sex education in schools. Unfortunately, notwithstanding all the twaddle about freedom of speech, this duty is rarely performed, or even acknowledged. Because of human respect, moral cowardice and the fear of getting involved, many remain silent when they should raise their voices. I could tell you much about my sad experience in such matters, when people were silent who should have spoken out. On the other hand, however, there are many occasions in which a man has no right to say even what he believes to be true or even to tell certain facts that he knows, because his speaking may have catastrophic consequences for other persons.

Again, when someone lacks all qualifications to say something true and deep, something good and important, his right to speak—his claim to freedom of speech—becomes rather dubious. Granted that no one has the right to stop him by force from satisfying his loquacity or from enjoying his alleged brilliance; still his speaking is a nuisance. One can only wish that a loving consideration for his fellow man would deter him from filling the air or newspapers or books with his drivel. Of such bores, Kierkegaard says in his witty way: "Having refused to use their freedom of thought, men claim freedom of speech as a compensation."

Now academic freedom is still much more relative than freedom of speech. It refers to the right to teach, in an institution of higher learning, everything that one considers to be true. This right is by its very nature limited in many respects. First, it is based on a contract between the institution and the teacher. Since the institution engages the professor, allows him to teach in its frame and pays him, the institution obviously has an important word to speak, as one partner in a bilateral contract.

A Crucial Distinction

We must make a crucial distinction at this point, namely between institutions of higher learning administered by the State, and those founded and run by private or religious interests.

Consider the situation in state-controlled colleges or universities; there should be no limitations concerning the convictions of the teacher; he should be able to teach in his class what he considers to be true. Here academic freedom should be respected. Given that a man has fulfilled the necessary requirements and that he possesses the usual intellectual stature, he has the right to expect that he will be considered for appointment to a State institution; and he has the right to teach what he thinks to be true when he is so appointed. His appointment should be rejected or terminated only for immoral behavior or because he is an agent of a political organization and thus lacks responsibility towards the State and toward the meaning and purpose of an institution of higher learning.

But consider a private college or university that, as a community, has a religious basis. It is obviously no longer possible for a man to claim the right to teach, in this frame, things that sap the very purpose of the institution. It is sheer nonsense for him to appeal to academic freedom as somehow entitling him to violate the freedom and the rights of the community that appointed him.

Freedom for a Community

If academic freedom has any sense, it applies not only to individual teachers, but also to any community that has founded a university on the basis of a particular conviction. No individual is forced to enter this university, whether as a student or as a professor. If a man does not share the same religious beliefs and all the consequences implied by this particular religion or *Weltanschauung* [world-view], he is perfectly free to go elsewhere.

I myself would never apply for a position at Yeshiva University, because I fully respect the right of the Jewish people to conduct a university based on their faith. Since I am a Catholic, I know I have no right to act as professor in a Jewish framework. It is unpardonable to teach under the cover of academic freedom things that are antithetical to the very basis and *raison d'être* of the institution and that even aim at sapping it. Such teaching would clearly infringe upon the right of the institution in question.

The above obviously applies to teaching only in those domains which, by their very nature, can be incompatible with a religious conviction. Such a domain is, above all, philosophy, and in a less direct way, sociology, psychology, anthropology and history. A professor of Romance languages or of chemistry need not be a Catholic in order to teach in a Catholic university. If he is engaged by a Catholic university, he can teach without any problem of limiting his academic freedom.

But even in such cases, in which a field offers no possible conflict with the *Weltanschauung* of a university as long as the professor does not infiltrate a dilettante philosophizing into his teaching, there always remains the fact that a teacher willingly or not also exerts an important influence on his students by his personality. His influence is in many cases not restricted to teaching in the strict sense of the word; the professor's personality also can emanate a strong atmosphere which is formed by his own *Weltanschauung*. He can kindle a personal attraction on the part of some of his students which draws them in the direction of his personal convictions.

And, above all, there is no field of teaching in which one cannot inject his *Weltanschauung* by way of informal asides. A professor of Latin, in dealing with the works of St. Augustine, can ridicule his faith; a professor of French can, by praising Voltaire, Camus and Sartre, and by tearing to pieces Leon Bloy, Claudel and Bernanos, insert all kinds of anti-religious and anti-Catholic ideas into what is overtly a lesson in French.

Nevertheless, we must make a clear distinction here. As long as the topic is as such neutral as to any *Weltanschauung*—a language or mathematics or chemistry—there is objectively no possible conflict with the convictions on which the Catholic university is based. In principle, therefore, a man can teach such topics even if he is not Catholic, granted only that he is a tactful person, who will not abuse his position by inserting anti-Catholic remarks, which obviously do not belong objectively to the topic of his teaching. But if the topic in question is essentially a *Weltanschauung*, or if it tacitly presupposes some philosophical position, the individual teacher who does not share the strictly Catholic world-view should not try to become a member of the teaching staff of a Catholic university. Nor should the university try to engage him. Once he is a member of the university, however, regardless of how this came about, he must respect the aim and purpose of the institution. Above all, the head of the university is morally obligated to ensure that his staff's teaching is not incompatible with Christian revelation. The president of a Catholic university has the duty to dismiss a professor as soon as his teaching clashes with the doctrine of the Church.

Freedom of Philosophy in a Catholic Framework

Still, even in philosophy there is plenty of leeway for a variety of positions that are in no way incompatible with the deposit of Catholic faith. Even though only one of these positions can be true (or in case these positions do not contradict one another, one may be more adequate and correct), they do not clash with the implicit presuppositions of Catholic faith. Whether a philosopher is a follower of Descartes or of St. Thomas, whether—like St. Thomas—he endorses Aristotle's epistemology, or whether he is convinced with St. Augustine that not all knowledge can be traced back to sensation, there is no incompatibility of any of these positions with the deposit of Catholic faith.

When it comes to teaching the history of philosophy, those philosophical systems which are indeed basically incompatible with the Catholic faith (such as Hume, Kant, Hegel, Heidegger or Dewey), should of course be thoroughly discussed. Yet, they should never be presented as true. After a clear and fair and accurate presentation of their contents, the grave errors they contain should be unmasked and refuted by *purely rational arguments.*

But everyone who has a minimum of intelligence (and this should be expected from teachers, instructors or professors) should be able to understand that it is intellectually dishonest to spread philosophical theories in a Catholic university that are incompatible with the doctrine of the Church. Such are all brands of relativism, immanentism, subjectivism, materialism and atheism, and any philosophy tainted with these errors. To present those theories as true is in fact to defraud the students.

Betrayers of the Faith

The pseudo-heroes of academic freedom eulogized in the *New York Times* are not outsiders—that is non-Catholics who enter a Catholic university. They are rather Catholics who have more or less lost their faith and who now try to spread their heretical ideas in the frame of a Catholic university. What in the case of a non-Catholic would be tactless behavior assumes here the character of a clear-cut betrayal. This betrayal reaches its climax in the case of priests or religious. It is especially with regard to these Catholic professors that the discussion about academic freedom rages.

The Right to Defend Belief

We must again insist that if the individual person has the right to utter his conviction, the community also possesses the same right. The very same principle which makes the State allow the teaching of different and antithetical doctrines in State universities, entitles any private university adhering to a religious creed to forbid the teaching of any doctrine opposed to the basic tenets of the institution.

In a Catholic university, as we noted before, it is the duty of the president or the dean to watch that nothing is taught as true that is incompatible with Christian revelation. Excluded, therefore, would be all branches of relativism, materialism, atheism, determinism and immanentism. In excluding these errors, the university simply makes use of its collective right of academic freedom in order to serve and protect the truth for which alone it exists—the truth which is its very *raison d'être*.

The claim of academic freedom assumes a completely ludicrous character when it is appealed to by Catholic theologians. Unlike metaphysics, theology is a field referring to truths inaccessible to our reason; by its very nature, therefore, theology is based on faith, and Catholic theology is based exclusively on the Catholic Faith. As soon as theologians place themselves outside this faith and outside of Christian revelation, the very object of theology vanishes, and it is replaced by imaginative constructions.

There is still another question at the basis of the whole discussion on academic freedom.

Many claim that universities based on a religious creed have no right to exist. Is not a Catholic university *ab ovo* prejudiced? Does not the claim of being scientific and objective belong to the very meaning and essence of a university, and does this not exclude the presupposition of a *Weltanschauung?*

Even Atheism Has Its *Weltanschauung*

To these arguments I respond: given that a religious creed is considered to be a prejudice that is incompatible with the scientific character of a university, it would be a gross naiveté to overlook the fact that atheism and agnosticism are as much *Weltanschauung*s as are religious creeds. The denial of something, after all, is no less dogmatic than a positive affirmation of it. To the ultimate questions of God's existence and of His revelation, there is no possibility of a complete neutrality: whether he knows it or not, every man is basically turned either toward God or against Him.

It would be easy to show how in many parts of so-called scientific research the influence of a certain *Weltanschauung* plays a great role. I do not think now of natural science, but of history, anthropology, psychology and sociology. Unproved, tacitly presupposed philosophical theories are the real, most dangerous prejudices that gravely compromise any objective research into scientific truth. Today we witness a frightening ascendancy of fashionable pseudo-philosophies in the fields of sociology and anthropology—an influence which is due only to the dynamism of the ideas now filling the air. The tacit acceptance of such ideas is certainly most unscientific and unobjective.

Pride Cripples Objectivity

We must now go further. It is not only uncritically accepted ideas and unproved theories that can prejudice the results of objective scientific inquiry. There are also many general attitudes in man that can influence his knowledge in an illegitimate way. Not only intelligence and intellectual talents are required in order to attain accurate scientific results, but also thoroughness, patience and honesty—none of which are intellectual perfections. They are rather general attitudes of men, implying moral elements.

Pride also distorts the objectivity of knowledge. This applies specifically to philosophy. In order to grasp being adequately, a man must approach reality with wonder. He must listen reverently to the voice of being; he must really seek truth and truth alone. He must possess the readiness to accept evident or strictly proven facts. He must be free from the bias created by pride, which is always eager to offer something "new" and "unheard-of."

A man's pride tempts him to construct a world according to its own liking. It allows him to consider philosophy as a field where he can show off his sophisticated reasoning—a field that grants him the occasion of displaying his brilliance and superiority over others. The great errors in philosophy, such as materialism, epistemological and moral relativism, skepticism, immanentism, subjectivism, determinism and atheism, are not caused by any intellectual deficiency, but rather by pride and several other general moral attitudes.

Skepticism is very fashionable today; so are all forms of relativism, including historical and cultural relativism, which claim that everything—every truth and every value— is time-bound. Such an intellectual attitude deeply reflects, and flows from, a type of pride which cannot stand the limits set to our arbitrariness. An absolute truth to which we must submit, which we should respect, to which our mind must conform, seems intolerable to this pride. Nietzsche describes this attitude well; and his own philosophy serves, amusingly enough, as a striking example.

Spiritual Laziness

Another attitude that paralyzes our knowledge is a sort of indolence, a spiritual laziness that is the refusal to "conspire" with the object and its nature. We refuse to move spiritually to the position that alone allows the nature of certain things to disclose themselves. This is the attitude of a spiritual obstinacy, which is at the very root of all materialism. The materialist looks only in one direction and credits reality only to beings that are accessible in this one direction.

Our knowledge can also be compromised by a habitual distrust, a fear of relying on the voice of being, of making the act of transcendence which all knowledge implies. It is an attitude similar to moral scrupulosity, or to the one of a man who always goes back to see whether he really has locked his car. We find this distrust in philosophy when men keep asking for a criterion of knowledge even when facing evident facts. They demand a criterion for the evidence! We have all met people who keep asking us the very same question in the course of a conversation. They wish some advice on the question of whether they should accept or refuse an offer. We give them a clear answer. After three minutes, they ask again: "So you really think I should accept?" And this goes on and on. This distrust and inhibition of transcending oneself is also at the basis of many forms of immanentism.

Irreverence Paralyzes and Distorts

Many more of these habitual attitudes might be noted which paralyze and distort our capacity for an unprejudiced, objective knowledge and which bring men to construct false theories. But time allows us to mention only one more, a specifically disastrous attitude. We mean *irreverence*. This is the basic incapacity to listen; it is the attitude that already knows everything before being has the opportunity to inform us. Irreverence is the impertinent, arrogant attitude that makes our minds deaf and blind to reality—the more so, the deeper and more sublime the object. All authentic philosophical knowledge requires reverence. Otherwise, the philosopher indulges in arbitrary constructions or even in a superficial chatter, and remains ignorant of the real nature of the being in question.

It should now be clear that the claim of the liberal university to an unprejudiced and unbiased approach is a great illusion. As soon as philosophical questions are at stake, as well as the philosophical presuppositions of many sciences, the idea that the liberal university—in contradistinction to a Catholic university—is free from all presuppositions, and is therefore unprejudiced, is a great error. Thus the argument that denies the right of a Catholic university to exist as a genuine university collapses as soon as we take the trouble to analyze more minutely the notion of "unprejudiced."

The Advantages of a Catholic University

But there is still much more to say in favor of a Catholic university. From the mere point of view of objective, unprejudiced knowledge, the Catholic university has a specific advantage. The general attitudes of reverence, humility, spiritual and mental alertness, readiness to conform to the nature of the being in question, and the trust in being—spiritual courage—are precisely attitudes which the Catholic faith evokes and develops in those who really live up to it. These are precisely the attitudes that liberate our knowledge. They do away with the prejudices that, as we saw, undermine, distort and paralyze our knowledge.

True Knowledge Is Unprejudiced

Let it now be emphatically stated: True knowledge must be unprejudiced. In his search, no man must presume to rest knowledge upon facts that are incapable of standing the test of reason. No Catholic philosopher, therefore, can deduce metaphysical truths from the content of revelation. As far as philosophy is concerned, he will accept only what he can grasp with his reason. The result of his research is not determined by his faith; nor is the resultant knowledge dependent upon the will or attitude of the knower.

A knower must assume the right attitude in order to grasp a thing as it is, to let it speak without interference. In this sense, certain wrong attitudes do indeed influence the result of inquiry, paralyzing our capacity for the transcending contact with being that true knowledge implies. They undermine the listening and hearing of the voice of being, and thus lead to intellectual errors. But the attitudes that are antithetical to these wrong attitudes do not influence the content of our knowledge. Rather they liberate knowledge from these distorting fetters and enable it to be exclusively determined by the nature of the being which is the object of our research.

Thus the opposites of pride and irreverence—humility and reverence—do not determine the content of our knowledge, but rather enable knowledge to complete in an unbiased way its mission: to grasp the object as it is, to conform our minds to the object. Similarly, the opposite of spiritual indolence or obstinacy—a certain winged alertness of the mind—follows the cue given by the object; is led by it; and is able to vibrate in unison with its *ratio*. This liberating alertness enables our intellect to recognize many objects in their true nature and to do justice to them. It widens the range of our intellect, opening our eyes for a reality which eludes the mentally obstinate attitude, the "stick in the mud" laziness.

Liberating Our Capacity for Knowledge

Equally does the antithesis of the metaphysical distrust and fear of transcendence—the metaphysical courage and faith—liberate our capacity for knowledge, for the very contact with being. We find ourselves willing to embark upon the great venture of letting ourselves be carried along by things. The same attitude that does not shrink from moral responsibility will also meet things without the prejudice of distrust, which dims the vision for evidence and for the difference between what is and what it not evident. It is an unbiased, trusting attitude, which does not render a man uncritical or gullible but merely enables him to take that step essential to understanding. It opens his eyes and ears.

Now it is not difficult to see that the attitude toward being created by Catholic dogma in a person who lives in a world such as is opened to us by Christian revelation, is precisely characterized by the fundamental features which deliver our knowledge, which clear away all the hindrances to knowledge, and which produce the type of mind capable of doing justice to the depth and range of reality. The Catholic faith actualizes in the soul of man reverence, humility, spiritual alertness, the thirst for truth, the metaphysical courage, the readiness to listen to the voice of being and to conform to it unreluctantly, the readiness to submit to the majesty of reality, and to vibrate with the specific *logos* of a thing. In a word: the Catholic faith actualizes a real transcendence and objectivity.

The True Catholic Attitude

The true Catholic is, to quote St. Bonaventure, "a man of desire like Daniel," and the true Catholic attitude is one of humility, free from all *ressentiment*, ready to submit and to serve; it is metaphysically courageous, healthy, undisgruntled, believing. I say the Catholic attitude, not the attitude of the average Catholic. We may be told, not without justification, that many of the great philosophers of antiquity such as Plato or Aristotle or those of modern times, such as Leibniz or Kierkegaard, were far more endowed with this attitude—were more "catholic" in this respect—than many Catholic thinkers. But if many Catholic thinkers lacked these attitudes which liberate man's knowledge in all philosophically relevant questions, it is precisely because they were not Catholic enough, because they were not formed as personalities by the Christian revelation. Indeed, they have looked up with excessive awe and undue respect to their liberal colleagues. They have let themselves be imprisoned by the liberal illusion of "unprejudice." Their pattern or ideal was determined rather by the liberal approach of non-Catholics.

But a truly Catholic university is not merely incompatible with "unprejudiced" inquiry. As far as philosophy and the philosophical presuppositions of certain other sciences are concerned, a Catholic university has an edge over all others.

If we realize the never ending conflict between the spirit of the world and the spirit of Christ; if we grasp the sacred mission entrusted to the Church, namely, to spread divine revelation in Christ and through Christ, and to protect this revelation along with the basic natural truths which this revelation implicitly presupposes, then we can clearly grasp the ignominious betrayal committed by those Catholic universities, colleges and schools that allow many things to be taught within their walls in blatant contradiction of faith. Such a practice is not only a self-condemnation of these institutions, not only a betrayal of their *raison d'être*, it is much worse: it is a betrayal of Christ; it is an apostasy masked by the slogan of "academic freedom."

If the rulers of such institutions have themselves lost their faith, their only honest action would be to close down the institutions—whether schools or high schools, or colleges, or universities. In so doing they would at least no longer defraud Catholic students by sponsoring the spread of heresies disguised as authentic Catholic learning. But if by this they would cease to be dishonest, they do not thereby cease to betray the mission entrusted to them by Christ: they are and remain apostates.

The Cowardice of Hirelings

In general, however, the heads of Catholic institutions do not prohibit the teaching of heresies not because they have definitely lost their faith, but because they yield to public opinion and to fashion. They fear to be called "reactionaries." They shudder at the thought of violating this allegedly holy academic freedom. Of these St. Augustine says:

Who is the hireling who, seeing the approach of the wolf, takes flight? He who seeks himself and does not seek what is of Jesus Christ; he who does not dare to frankly admonish the sinner (1 Tim. 5:20). See, someone has sinned, gravely sinned; he should be admonished, excluded from the Church. But, excluded from the Church, he will become its enemy and will try to ensnare it and harm it where he can. Now the hireling, the one who seeks himself and not what is of Jesus Christ, will be silent and will not give any admonition, in order not to lose what he seeks, namely the advantages of personal friendship, and in order to avoid the unpleasantness, worry and personal enmity. The wolf at that moment takes hold of the sheep to throttle them....You are silent O hireling, and do not admonish....Your silence is your flight. You are silent, you are afraid. Fear is the flight of the soul. (St. Augustine, *Tractatus in Joannem*, XLVI, 7-8.)

XIII

The Illusion of Progress

Many people pride themselves on being "progressive." Many rejoice in the progress the world has achieved in the twentieth century. To strive for the progress of humanity is considered by innumerable persons as the most noble and selfless and important aim. It is worthwhile, therefore, to ask ourselves what "progress" means, and of what it consists.

Progress is more than mere growth. Progress has the connotation of a growth of something positive. To be correct, we should not speak of progress with respect to an infectious disease which gets worse, or spreads more and more. The opposite of progress is not only a regression but also the growth and spread of an evil.

A mere neutral growth or development is also not yet progress. Real progress requires an ascension, a development leading the way upward to the better or more perfect.

Another important distinction is whether progress is to be found only in a certain field or whether we can speak of progress with respect to man's life as a whole, to the fulfillment of his destiny, to the very meaning and *raison d'être* of his life.

119

In asserting that there has been progress in a certain field, we have in no way answered the question of whether this progress is a real good for man as a whole, whether it really makes his life happier and whether it is a benefit from the point of view of his sanctification and his eternal beatitude. We must distinguish between progress in a certain domain and its relationship to absolute progress. Absolute progress must be measured according to the words of Christ: "What does it profit a man to gain the whole world and suffer the loss of his soul?" Thus religious and moral progress, in the soul of an individual, constitutes the only absolute progress. This progress, however, does not take place by itself as our physical growth does; it presupposes man's free will, his free collaboration with God's grace. St. Augustine said, "He who made thee without thee does not justify thee without thee." This progress is absolute insofar as it refers to the *unam necessarium*: the one thing necessary; and all progress in other fields can be deemed authentic only as long as it furthers, or at least does not prevent, this absolute progress.

But it is also necessary to ask whether all the progress in certain fields, in technology, for instance, in chemistry and in astronomy, is also progress in respect to the beauty, depth and true happiness of human life. The last word always has to be: does it glorify God, does it lead man further on the way to sanctification? But also the question must be asked: does any development make man really more happy on earth, does it make his life richer, deeper, healthier; and this question also has precedence over all imminent progress in a certain field.

One thing must be emphatically stressed, however: there are certain fields in which progress is more or less automatic; for example, in the natural sciences, medicine and technology; but in other fields, such an automatic progress is definitely not to be found. Neither in art, nor in philosophy, nor in culture in general (as distinct from civilization), is there any automatic evolution. The Hegelian theory of a continual development in history, that is an increasing unfolding of the *Weltgeist* (the world spirit), in no way corresponds to reality.

At this point, we must distinguish between two different illusions. First, the one of a more philosophical order—the illusion that there is a continual development upward. This is the fatal Hegelian error of an increasing unfolding of the *Weltgeist*. Certainly, the Hegelian does not consider it a simple ascension, but he does think it takes place according to a rhythm of thesis, antithesis and synthesis. But the synthesis, according to this theory, necessarily ranks higher than both thesis and antithesis. This theory of an imminent automatic progress of humanity is an Hegelian "invention."

The second illusion refers not to a general thesis, to a law dominating the universe and especially the history of mankind, but the concrete thesis about a fact. It is the illusion of the wonderful progress of our epoch, the enthusiasm about its superiority which manifests itself in the slogan, "Today, man has come of age."

This second illusion entails an absolute blindness to the terrible decay taking place today in the most important fields of human life. It is difficult to understand how anyone unprejudiced and intelligent can be blind to the rapid decay, the disintegration, the demoralization and especially the dehumanization that we witness day by day. But it is more than difficult; it is thoroughly appalling that even Catholic priests, bishops and cardinals are blind to this decay and exhibit an unwarranted optimism.

With the triumph of technology that began in the machine era, beauty was more and more replaced by comfort. If civilization pursues ease in practical life and efficiency in reaching practical ends; and if culture, an impractical superabundance, merely enriches and elevates human life; then civilization has throttled culture. Since the early nineteenth century, the earth has been more and more ruined. The beauty of nature has been jeopardized by horrible looking factories. Railways, machines of all kinds, advertisements, they all undermine more and more the deep and sublime poetry of nature. The elementary importance of beauty as spiritual nourishment of the soul is no longer understood.

A particularly disastrous aspect of this throttling of culture has been the progressive downfall of architecture in the past fifty years. We have followed the pseudo-Gothic monsters of the end of the last century with an architecture adapted to the prosaic, depersonalized life, the mechanized, pragmatical life. We have devastated our towns and nature itself by these monster buildings, apartment houses and factories characterized by an absolute anonymity, a soulless, endlessly boring note and a continuous repetition.

Under the illusion that architecture was beautiful if it satisfied practical needs, under the illusion of this unfortunate functionalism, we forgot that man is above all a person, that the apartment in which he lives is not only important for his health, for his practical needs, it is also the place in which his life as a person displays itself, in which he contacts other persons, in which he loves and prays. And thus the beauty of the room, of the apartment or house in which a man lives is also an important factor for the nourishment of his soul; it should be a harbor of his life, a frame that corresponds in its atmosphere to the beautiful and deep things in his life.

And nobody who is unprejudiced, and not infected by this arbitrary and delusional preference for his own epoch, can overlook the radical decline of the fields of music and fine arts. You need only compare the music of Bach, Gluck, Mozart, Beethoven, Schubert, Wagner, Brahms, Bruckner and Verdi with atonal or electronic music to see the abyss which separates the music of our day from the riches of the past. Or compare today's abstract painting, or the paintings of Picasso, with a Titian, Michelangelo, Reubens, Rembrandt, Renoir or Cézanne. Is this total disrespect of nature, this pseudo-originality, not deeply symptomatic of the revolt against form and of the love of chaos?

The eminent role that beauty plays in the life of man, not only for his happiness, not only for drawing his mind upward but even for his mental health has more and more been forgotten, although Bruno Bettelheim did recognize the influence of beauty on mental health to the extent of using beautiful drawings as a cure for mental sickness in his Chicago clinic. The replacement of beauty by comfort and efficiency, the de-poetization of man's life, brings about a dehumanization, a human atrophy, even if the average man is not aware of it.

Culture has been throttled by civilization. More and more it is believed that learning is the real sign of culture. The more someone has learned, the more degrees he has, the more is he considered cultured. This is a great error.

The artisan in Florence in the fifteenth century possessed a high culture even if he could not read or write. His culture manifested itself in his personality, in the way he expressed himself, and in the sense of beauty in his work. Until a hundred years ago in Italy, in many places around Florence, the old peasant sang a song of the *Divina Commedia* of Dante by heart in the evening to his family and to all those who worked for him, although he could not read or write. It was a living tradition. This is the real man of culture—not the man who has been stuffed with knowledge of all sorts, who has been distorted by false philosophies, who has lost all of the genuine charm and unpretentiousness of the simple man, whose relation to everything in life has become second-hand.

Everyone who knows what real culture is cannot but observe its continuous decline: the triumph of uniformism and of the gregarious instinct; the anonymous crowd replaces more and more the individual personality.

The decline of philosophy is at least equally terrible. The fashionable followers of positivism, of materialism, of Heidegger, may differ technically but they are equally dreary; and they all share epistemological and moral relativism. The slogan, "there is no objective truth," is their dogmatic basis. Instead of truth they offer a kind of historical, sociological notion of the "life of an idea" which at certain times makes headway and has influence; but it has nothing to do with truth.

Real truth lives forever; but the object of modern philosophy is a Mayfly in the air which has a kind of historical, sociological reality that is presented as the more important thing. We cannot insist too strongly on the ridiculous self-contradiction of their denial of objective truth and of all transcendence. It suffices to realize how the propagation of these self-contradictory and mediocre theories murders the common sense of the greatest part of the students in our universities and colleges and how such intellectual superstition threatens to dehumanize their healthy approach to life.

Worse yet, in terms of the number of souls at risk, an unheard-of amoralism is rapidly spreading. There have always been sins against the sixth commandment. There always were people who yielded to the temptations of the flesh; but they either knew that their actions were immoral and even felt contrition about their sin, or at least, if they were really frivolous and impure, they still wanted to hide it. They had still an indirect recognition of the immorality of impurity. But today's absolute amoralism is completely blind to the horror of impurity. It is the death of all bashfulness, which even the pagans possessed; it is actually the neutralization of this domain. Let us not forget that hypocrisy is something hideous. Amorality is incomparably worse.

Sex education in the classroom forces this amorality on innocent children; its caricature of sex in the name of science destroys its role as a great source of happiness in human life. It deprives sex of its character of mystery, its intimacy, and misrepresents it as something merely biological, such as digestion.

And this is done over the heads of the inalienable rights of parents. Is this not totalitarianism? So is the proposed parents' certification for procreation; and so is the notion that a bank of sperm and artificial insemination—this horrible inhumanity—will assume the role that God has given to marriage. Can you imagine a worse nightmare than this disrespect for man's dignity and his freedom? Away with all intimacy, and all faith in providence! Man has now come so much of age and has such wisdom that he can take the role of God. Moral law aside, this is the condemnation to an endless, absolute boredom. All the charm and happiness of love and parenthood presuppose the phenomena of gift and surprise. People have forgotten this.

Worst of all, everywhere we hear of the admirable progress in what concerns the dignity of man and his freedom in democratic countries. But to treat man like a figure on a chessboard, to direct him over his head and without regard for his free will, implies a deeper disrespect for human dignity than all political tyranny in former times. The brainwashing of people through the mass media, in advertising and political propaganda renders the right to vote a very doubtful freedom. A great majority is influenced by the mass media, and by the money that puts these media at the disposal of a minority.

Who is the fool who claims that humanity is progressing and who boasts about the glorious freedom man has reached, about the respect for the dignity of man and that the average man today has come of age? Let me state clearly that whoever enthuses about the progress of the 20th century, if he doesn't mean progress in a certain field of technology or medicine, etc., but the entirety human life, is either a fool or an instrument of the devil. The devil knows that "progress" is the slogan by which he can fool the idealists into following him and partaking unknowingly in his work of destruction.

But the illusion of progress has infected even the nominal enemies of the Devil: It has invaded the sanctuary of the Church. Teilhard de Chardin has introduced this mischievous illusion about the industrialized world, seeing in it a wonderful step in the process of evolution, and identifying automatic evolution with the process of history. And, unfortunately, this illusion of an automatic progress, a progress unfolding itself visibly in our present time, has gained currency in the mind of many priests, theologians, bishops and cardinals. Their alleged modern man is a pure myth, who has come of age and thus can no longer be expected to accept the plain doctrine of the Church, that is, the revelation of God. Should we not expect people formed and fed by the doctrine of the Church to grasp what common sense cannot overlook?

Not necessarily. First, there are the prelates who have not only lost their faith but who remain in the Church in order to destroy it. If I lost my faith, I would leave the Church. But to lose the faith and remain in the Church, there must be some reason for that. They use the slogan "progress" as a means to camouflage their diabolical work of destruction and to fool the faithful, in order to draw them away from Christ and His holy Church. They are real servants of the anti-Christ.

A second much larger group of prelates are the victims influenced by the accusation that the Church is reactionary, that She is blocking the progress of humanity. They have not enough intelligence, and not enough faith, to resist the brainwashing of the propagators of progress. Their inferiority complex makes them fear to miss the bandwagon and, thus, they also become champions of progress. They dare not protect their fold, for instance, from this horrible new invention of sensitivity training, one of the stupidest superstitions that ever existed in the world. They will yield to sex education in the classroom because, after all, it belongs to progress. If they did not accept it, people might believe that they were narrow-minded, prudish, not up to date; and that would the worst of all things.

A third type are those who are not infected by the myth of progress but who simply are afraid to become unpopular, afraid of being attacked in the liberal press, those who have not enough guts to make use of their authority as bishops and priests to call the progressive heresies by their true names, to intervene. They fear that they may lose all influence in their dioceses, or in their parishes; and they yield to the Senate of Priests in their dioceses, to the alleged majority vote of their parish councils. They fear to forbid books and magazines in the bookracks that are infected with heretical ideas, refined attempts to undermine the real faith; and they dare not display good, orthodox books. They follow an ostrich policy. They minimize the danger. They close their eyes.

And finally, there are many very pious priests and bishops who are deeply depressed about the disintegration of faith, about the loss of the sense of the supernatural, of sanctity and holy love. But they fear that by fighting they may disturb the alleged peace among Catholics.

Hand in hand with the illusion of progress goes the most fatal disease ravaging the Church: this-worldliness. By this-worldliness I mean the emphasis on the amelioration of this world and the earthly welfare of man in contradistinction to the glorification of God and the eternal welfare of man. According to this deplorable error, the Church should now concern Herself above all with the social order, with social justice, peace among nations and ecumenism, instead of the sanctification of the individual soul and the glorification of God through the conversion of all men to Christ and His holy Church.

This-worldliness combines the blindness to the terrible decline of humanity with the confusion o belief in the imminent progress in the world leading to the realization of the reign of Christ. The champions of this-worldliness speak much in their new catechisms of social justice, of pacificism and anti-Colonialism, of progress in natural science; they skip the Ten Commandments and say as little as possible about sin, hell, purgatory, contrition, penance, the transformation in Christ and eternal beatitude.

But Christ has never spoken about the institutions of this world, nor about the progress of this world, but about the conversion of all men to God, their redemption and sanctification, and above all of the glorification of God. He has spoken about the terrible punishment for those who persist in disobedience until death, and He has spoken about the glory of eternal beatitude. The establishment of the reign of Christ is just the opposite of this belief in an imminent progress of this world and the spirit of this-worldliness.

Has Christ not stressed the indirect, considerable antagonism between His message and the spirit of the world? "Had you been of the world, the world would have loved you. But you are not of the world; the world hates you." And this will remain true until the last day of this world.

No, the real mission of the Church is not to strive for an earthly paradise, not to humanize the world together with atheists and communists, but to establish the reign of Christ in every individual soul.

The great Cardinal Newman, whom we need more than ever today, has said:

Saint Paul...labored more than all the Apostles: and why? Not to civilize the world, not to smooth the face of society...not to spread abroad knowledge, not to cultivate the reason, not for any great worldly object...not to turn the whole earth into a heaven, but to bring down a heaven upon earth. This has been the real triumph of the Gospel....It has made men saints.

And this great and holy mission of the Church is indissolubly linked with the condemnation of all heresies, with the glorious anathema by which the Church overcame all attempts of the Devil to undermine it. When the great fighter against the modernist heresies, St. Pius X, chose as his motto the admirable words *instaurare omnia in Christo*, "to renew everything in Christ," he did not mean that we ought to make of the earth a natural paradise, an ideal of a world in harmony and peace, freed from all kinds of illness and poverty, a humanity gaining always more natural empirical knowledge and a greater domination over nature. No, he meant transfiguring everything that we do by the spirit of Christ, transforming all natural values such as human love, marriage, family, cultural life, art, politics, natural truths, in Christ whereby their most intimate value will shine forth; but even above and more than that, something completely new is added—the holy breath of Christ. A mere imminently perfect world—if we may assume such an impossible fiction for a moment—a world in which all people were friendly and naturally kind, a world without illness, wars and poverty, but in which no one would adore God, no one would bend his knee before Christ, would have no right to exist for a moment; it would be an abomination.

If in former times, many Catholic priests and bishops sometimes did not appreciate enough the true natural goods, it was certainly deplorable. Some ten years ago, I said: "Every true Catholic should manifest his faith also by seeing every high, natural good, such as human love, marriage, beauty in nature and art, natural truth in its true authentic value, in appreciating it more than anyone without faith."

But it is infinitely worse when representatives of the Church forget to preach the *unam necessarium* and promote natural goods only, and when they interpret the message of Christ as a program for establishing an earthly paradise. In the moment in which the absolute primacy of the one thing necessary is no longer seen, everything is falsified; and even true, natural goods are deprived of their authentic beauty and value.

I have always fought the false supernaturalism of those who say, when someone loses a beloved person, "Oh, don't worry too much; if he died well, then there is no reason to worry and, moreover, he is much happier now." No, the great natural goods which God bestows on us should evoke our deep gratitude towards Him and we should rejoice about them and enjoy them. The crosses that God lays on our shoulders should deeply affect us: we should worry, we should mourn, we should weep, but say, "Thy will be done."

St. Bernard wrote a wonderful sermon (No. 26 in his sermons on the Canticle of Canticles) mourning the death of his beloved brother, who was also a monk in the same monastery. Here we find the right response: deep suffering over the death of his brother in a man whose gaze was fixed only on the one thing necessary. Precisely because St. Bernard saw the absolute primacy of the supernatural, he was in the fullest and highest sense human and reacted in the deepest and most adequate way to earthly goods and crosses. He understood that the deaths of people we love call for tears—*sunt lacrimae rerum,* as Virgil said.

Everything on this earth reveals its true value only when it is seen in the light of eternity, only when we understand that this life is a *status viae* [pilgrimage] destined to find its fulfillment in eternity, only when we grasp that we are pilgrims directed toward eternity. In Christ every true natural good reveals its true beauty, *in lumine tuo videbimus lumen* (in your light, we shall see light), but precisely because only in Him are all natural goods understood as a message of God destined to draw us nearer to Him, to enflame our heart for Him. It is only when these natural goods do not claim to be the last fulfillment, only when they profess their incompleteness do they reveal their highest beauty and, in their beauty, God the absolute. To recognize the primacy of the supernatural with respect to the natural is essential for grasping the real beauty and value of natural goods. Only in Christ can we distinguish natural goods having a high value, such as friendship, marriage, natural truth, beauty in nature and art, from lower worldly goods, such as wealth and fame. This-worldliness, therefore, makes us blind to true natural values.

In order to overcome the intrusion of this-worldliness into the Church, we must free ourselves from the illusion of progress. We must also condemn its corollary blindness to the decline and regression of our epoch, and the superstition about attaching ourselves to the present in order to love our neighbor and avoid a melancholic nostalgia for former times. If we restore in our souls the primacy of the supernatural and the true vision of all natural goods in Christ, we shall understand the terrible decay, the regress of this moment in humanity, and the terrible danger to which the holy Church is exposed by the intrusion of this-worldliness. But facing all that, we can live as pilgrims, our hearts filled with hope, not optimism, with hope primarily for our own and our brothers' eternal union with Christ—and with hope for the glorious reign of Christ in the Church.

We should realize that the situation of the Church today is similar to the one prevalent in the fourth century, when the majority of Catholic bishops were Arians. But St. Anathanius and St. Hilarius of Poitiers, together with orthodox laymen, saved the Church from heresy.

Inside the Church today, and outside it, many consider peace the primary aim of our striving: peace among nations, peace with the communists, peace with the heretics, *peace with the spirit of the world*. Certainly, Christ has said: Blessed are the peacemakers; but He has also called us to the fight against the spirit of the world. And this fight will never cease as long as this world exists. We must be both peacemakers, and soldiers of Christ, members of the *militant* Church.

XIV

Confidence in the Holy Spirit

Why is it that progressive Catholics so often refer to the Holy Spirit? When Fr. Avery Dulles, S. J., writes that to resist changes in the doctrine of the Church "would betray a lack of confidence in the Holy Spirit," he is repeating a slogan one hears daily from those who wish to discard dogmas of the Faith. Another Jesuit, Fr. David Knight, even goes so far as to assert that the Holy Spirit animated the faculty rebellion against the authority of the bishops at Catholic University last Spring! Grammar-school catechisms are now telling children that moral commandments, including the Decalogue, should cease to play a role in Christian morality, but that the Christian should rather follow the inspiration of the Holy Spirit. And it is commonly suggested that the Holy Spirit speaks to us through "history," and through the mentality of our epoch.

One wonders how it is, in a time when the doctrines of the Trinity and the divinity of Christ are called into question, that the existence of the Holy Spirit seems to be in no way doubted; that, on the contrary, adaptation of the Church to the "scientific age" and denial of dogma are urged in the name of the Holy Spirit. Although the Holy Spirit is in fact

133

the Third Person of the Trinity, He is seemingly accepted as the one indubitable reality.

The exception from the general attack on traditional belief that is granted the Holy Spirit is especially surprising in view of the tendency among *avant garde* Catholics to accept the Gospel as the exclusive source of Christian faith; for what the Gospel reveals to us about the Holy Spirit is much less than what it reveals about God the Father and God the Son. But perhaps it is precisely because the nature of the Holy Spirit remains more mysteriously hidden that our progressive Catholics—those interested in replacing the deposit of Catholic faith with new theologies—masquerade as His champions. They find it easy to interpret Him according to their own caprice. Moreover, many make of the Holy Spirit a kind of Hegelian *Weltgeist,* by way of justifying a continuing revelation and, hence, a continual change in its content.

Others are finding it convenient to refer to the Holy Spirit while they eliminate moral commandments. Instead of an unpalatable obedience to univocal moral commandments, they urge that Christians rely exclusively on the inspiration of the Holy Spirit. With this flexible readiness to follow the Holy Spirit a man can feel quite pious, while he is in fact writing for himself a license to follow his own subjective preferences and views. This phenomenon has recurred throughout Christian history. Christian Gnostics have always emphasized the Holy Spirit. The Montanists, for example, who arose in the second century, claimed an authority superior to that of the Church because of their direct inspiration by the Holy Spirit. Joachim of Flora in the twelfth century prophesied that the age of the Son would be superseded by that of the Holy Spirit. And thus it is, also, with the twentieth-century descendants of this ancient sect.

Of course, to accuse those who protest against the denial of dogma of a lack of confidence in the Holy Spirit is really a sign of either simple-minded confusion or insincerity. The persons who make this accusation are playing the Holy Spirit off against the infallible magisterium of the Church. This can only mean that the voice of the Holy Spirit which we believed to be guiding the Church and which we thought could be heard in the *ex cathedra* decisions of the Church is actually to be found elsewhere. Has it been transferred to "history"? If so, on what source is this new "dogma" based? Did Christ in speaking of the Paraclete refer to the course of history? Or is the Holy Spirit assumed to manifest Himself today through a team of professors of theology? Or perhaps through the mind of such as Avery Dulles, S.J.?

In any case, the Holy Spirit in Whom we are told to have "confidence" as we give up our faith in the doctrines of the Church—doctrines the purity and integrity of which the faithful believed were protected through two thousand years by the Holy Spirit—is something completely vague and confusing. Do Fr. Dulles and the other partisans of "new opinions" ask us to believe that although the Holy Spirit did not guide the Church until the present decade, we should nevertheless have confidence that He will enlighten the "modernized" Church in the future? That, apparently, is their position; for, on the one hand, they consider the dogmas of the Faith mere human formulations, subject to error (and they do not hesitate to dismiss, for example, the dogma of the Virgin Birth of Christ); and, on the other hand, they have complete "confidence" in the Holy Spirit (Whose existence is, of course, also a dogma and therefore—according to their logic—subject to "error" and "change"). Who will guide the Church of tomorrow in which new dogmas will replace the old. Presumably, contradiction is the special sign of the progressives' "Holy Spirit."

Now, it is quite true that Catholics can lose faith in the Holy Spirit. But this happens precisely when they doubt the unchangeable truth of dogma; for this doubt indeed betrays a total lack of confidence in the guidance of the Church by the Holy Spirit. However, the confidence in the Holy Spirit which Avery Dulles and other progressive writers recommend is a blatant contradiction.

Fr. Dulles would say that since there is no "static truth," change in the essential teaching of the Church is the authentic manifestation of the working of the Holy Spirit. But the denial of "static truth" means that any argument, any discussion, any "confidence" can make no sense at all—even the confidence in the non-existence of static truth. Nowadays, it is unfortunately necessary to point out the ludicrous contradiction inherent in claiming truth—i.e., "static" truth, objective truth, truth in the only intelligible sense of the term—for the denial of truth. But quite apart from this sophomoric contradiction, what can the progressives' "confidence in the Holy Spirit" mean? How can one have confidence in someone whose existence is not guaranteed, who might not be believed in tomorrow when the "dynamic truth" undergoes another updating change?

Against the background of this impious playing with the name of the Holy Spirit one can see the speciousness in the Jesuit Bernard Lonergan's argument that, because no one is attempting to introduce a new Christ, there is today no religious crisis, only a philosophical and cultural one. But apostasy from Christ and His Holy Church does not require that one introduce a new Christ (although one can well doubt the identity of Teilhard's Christ and the Christ of the Gospel); one has only to avail oneself of the logical absurdity and rhetorical deception of claiming that one's "new theology" or "new opinion"—i.e., one's break with the doctrine Christ revealed to His Church to safeguard and to teach—is the very manifestation of the Holy Spirit.

XV

The Triumph of Mediocrity

The Nazis idolized race, and subordinated spiritual values to vital values, for a number of reasons; one interesting effect was that every insignificant and modestly gifted German could feel superior to any genius who happened to have some Jewish blood. Now, the phenomenon of Catholic progressivism, which is plaguing the Church today, is of course not an instance of racism; but it is just as much a revolt against spirituality of all sorts and it, too, represents a triumph of mediocrity. And in both cases there is an attempt to compensate for feelings of inferiority: in National-Socialist Germany the trick was proving that one had an Aryan grandmother; today, in the Catholic orbit, it is the claim of "up-to-datedness," of "revolutionary innovation," of having "come of age."

The speeches of Hans Küng and Eduard Schillebeeckx, the writings of Avery Dulles and John Sheerin, and so many articles in *America, Commonweal, The Catholic World* and other periodicals of the Catholic press, cannot fail to remind one who has heard or read them of the speeches and lectures that were delivered in Nazi Germany. There is the same preference for slogans, the same intellectual mediocrity, the same looking down on all the great, timeless contributions of former ages, the same illusion that a great new era has begun (the Nazis called it the "thousand-year Reich"; the Catholic progressives, the "postconciliar era"), the same irreverence, the same adolescent pride, the same self-congratulation at living in the present age, the same unfounded optimism.

But whereas in Nazi Germany the mediocrity was imposed by the Führer and his cooperators (and supported by many professors out of fear), the present eruption of mediocrity is taking place under the cover of democracy, freedom of speech and academic freedom. In both cases, however, one can observe the extreme contagion of mediocrity. And in both cases, the mass media are instruments for the brainwashing of society at large.

The present aggressive mediocrity is another instance of compensating for poverty of thought with emphatic, prolix and noisy expression. Our "modernists" are like youngsters going through the puberty crisis who pretend to understand everything, to be competent enough to comment on everything, who disdain all that has been considered venerable and true, who manage to feel quite original while repeating old errors. This is nothing but decking the greatest contingency and deep-seated insecurity with boasts of complete independence.

In this situation, slavish devotees of intellectual fashions pride themselves on being in the *avant garde*. Just as the young adolescent will assert his adulthood in order to feel important, so the mediocre theologians, professors, journalists and priests of our time expand their egos with the intellectual drugs of progressivism and "modernity." As the pubescent will often show off more the more he feels insecure, and will assert something more emphatically the less certain he is about it, so popular progressive intellectuals cover their mediocrity by saying outrageous things.

It suffices to read one page of St. Augustine, or Pascal, or Kierkegaard, or Newman to see the abyss separating these great minds from the mediocrity of such as Küng, Schillebeeckx, or Avery Dulles. All the posturing, all the bluffing of these rebels against tradition, cannot conceal their dense mediocrity. There is a legend of a visit Diogenes paid to Socrates. In order to show his independence from worldly desire, Diogenes wore a coat full of many holes. But Socrates said to him: "From every hole of thy coat peeps out thy vanity."

The ludicrousness of this triumph of mediocrity must not obscure for us its tragic aspect. The "slave revolt," as Nietzsche called the self-assertion of the mediocre, becomes incomparably repulsive and dangerous when it extends to the religious sphere. In the realm of faith, where everything is based on revelation, where only to the Church has the authentic doctrine of Christ been entrusted, the wild speculations of mediocre theologians can have terrible consequences.

Fr. Hans Küng is typical of the hyperactive progressive mediocrities. When he emphatically declares that every formulation in human concepts necessarily borders on error and that this is especially so in dogmatic formulations because of their polemical nature, and when he then goes on to affirm that Luther's *sola fides* theory is the true doctrine on justification, he presents a compound of contradictions while using the popular rhetorical technique in which a tone of aggressive confidence and certainty substitutes for logical demonstration. That was one of the special features of Hitler's speeches; and the power of this crude rhetorical trick should not be underrated. When Neville Chamberlain returned to England after Munich, he declared that a man who spoke with so much enthusiasm about peace could not be intending to wage war. The point here is not the fact of widespread deception, but rather the pervasive replacement of logical argument by energy and vigor of assertion, by the tone in which something is said, with a view to giving the impression that something self-evident has been put forward. This devaluation of content, this shift from meaning and truth to rhetoric is a typical weapon of the mediocre who wish to achieve a cheap importance.

To be sure, there exists also a harmless type of mediocrity which is content to remain in its modest place. But what we have faced in the Church in recent years is the revolution of the mediocre. Before the Second Vatican Council there were many theologians and priests who had no great culture, no profound intelligence, and even a mediocre approach to life; but they remained silent, or repeated by rote the glorious teaching of the Church. Perhaps they did so in an inadequate way, mechanically and superficially; but still they were poor mouthpieces of something incomparably greater than their own limited minds: they transmitted divine truth. They accepted a modest role. Their mediocrity was regrettable, but not disastrous. But when the mediocre aspires to be a creative mind, when he becomes a "revolutionary," when he is no longer satisfied with serving, when he is no longer protected by a frame of truth, then the same perversion of mind sets in that one witnessed in the German National Socialists. (Hitler was rightly called the hero of trash; he was also a hero of mediocrity.)

In the intense mediocrity that is known as "Catholic progressivism," the most mediocre layman, priest or professor of theology (being a professor is not the least insurance against the dullest mediocrity) now aspires to "reform" the Church, to create a "new theology," to be "revolutionary." The futile attempt of such persons to conceal the mediocrity of their thought appears, as we have said, in the substitution of a tone of passionate conviction for rational argument. It also appears in the dependence on slogans to brainwash the public. These slogans are as meaningless as they are (unhappily) efficacious. The anathema against heresies and heretics, for example, is currently labeled "a negative approach"; whereas the ostrich policy of closing one's eyes to the threat of heresy, or even considering heresies "interesting," "new" "contributions" is called "a positive approach." Yet, the slogans of "triumphalism" and "historical consciousness" justify the *denial*—and even furious polemics against—the Church's infallibility and the "static truth" of the dogmas as something "positive." People who substitute slogans for logic are not embarrassed by contradictions.

XVI

False Apologetics

There has always been a danger of falling into a fallacious apologetic of Christianity and the Catholic Church. I remember a professor of moral theology at the University of Freiburg in 1910 who, in order to put St. Thomas Aquinas in a favorable light in the eyes of the numerous adherents of capitalism, claimed that it was the Angelic Doctor who was really the father of capitalism and not Calvin as Max Weber had said. By "apologizing" thus the professor accepted the wrong norm of the children of the world. In order to attract them to the Church and Christianity, he tried to show that even from the point of view of their own standards, St. Thomas was to be praised. He hoped to prove that the Church could meet the test of worldly norms.

But such false apologetics remained the exception and never appeared in the official Catholic manuals or in the catechism. Today, however, an apologetic based on the standards of the world has unfortunately found its way into the seminaries, the Catholic colleges and high schools, and even the grammar schools; and, of course, one encounters it in many Catholic periodicals and newspapers. Although Pope Paul VI has solemnly warned against it in the encyclical

Ecclesiam Suam and in many allocutions, this mistaken apologetic continues to spread. Compared with the present growing acceptance of the standards and norms of the world, the example mentioned above is no more than an amusing trifle.

In the Church today, false apologists are adapting the Christian message to the spirit of the world to such an extent that they completely falsify the former. Their apology is in reality a flagrant betrayal of Christ. They have adjusted the Gospel to worldly norms and can communicate, therefore, only a distortion of the message of Christ. The children of the world are not being asked to convert, for they are not being called upon to surrender their anti-Christian terms. Of course, they are quite ready to accept a false Christ, a Christ who does not require them to set aside their false norms for the true ones, a Christ who is no longer a scandal to the world. Their Christianity can only be nominal. The end result of false apologetics is that instead of converting the non-Christians, the false apologists are themselves converted to non-Christian standards. These feeble laborers in the vineyard of the Lord often have a deeper motive than a desire to win non-Christians to the Church. Many falsify the message of Christ and the doctrine of the Church because they are so impressed by non-Catholic criticism of the Church that they measure and judge themselves by its standards.

One can distinguish three kinds of criticism of the Church.

The first is based on false, worldly standards. This criticism blames the Church for those features for which it actually deserves praise. For example, there are those both within and without the Church who are so scandalized by the sight of men placing holiness above efficiency that they accuse contemplative monks of being idle and irrelevant, and recommend that they perform some useful work for Society. This criticism is patently unjust because that which it blames is in fact most praiseworthy.

The second kind of criticism is founded on true principles, but is unjust, because it attributes to the Church things which, though objectively evil, are not to be found in it. Such is the criticism of those Protestants who claim that the Papacy is based on a human craving for power, that it is an outgrowth of a worldly spirit. If the Church were indeed guilty of this charge, the blame would be entirely justified. But this criticism is unjust, because it is based on a misunderstanding of the nature of the Papacy, on a confusion of the accidental faults of individual Popes with the Papacy as such.

The third type of criticism is neither founded on false norms nor unjust in its attributions. It rightly accuses the behavior and spirit of Catholics who fail to live up to the norms of Christian life—those who are infected with secularism or who yield to vice. Under this head, also, should be placed the criticism of real abuses that may be found even among the hierarchy of the Church.

Our concern here is with the first kind of criticism—the one that blames the Church for its holiness, for its supernatural spirit—the criticism based on the false norms and pseudo-values of the *civitas diaboli*. This criticism is currently making a great impression on many Catholics who are more eager to pass the world's test than Christ's. They take the world's criticism so seriously that they attempt to justify the Church by showing that even when judged against worldly standards the Church does not deserve this criticism. They have forgotten the words of Our Lord: "Had you been of the world, the world would love its own; but as you are not of the world, as I have chosen you out of the world, the world hates you." These Catholics fail to understand that the Church must always be a scandal to the world and that the proper refutation of the world's criticism, therefore, consists in the unmasking and open rejection of the false standards behind this criticism. Instead, they want to combine the message of Christ with the spirit of the world—an impossible undertaking. They feel uneasy on hearing the false criticism. They sometimes mistakenly believe that humility imposes on them the duty of taking this criticism at face value. They do not distinguish between criticism which refers to the worldly, secular, and sinful attitudes and activities of members of the Church and that criticism which itself originates in false, secular norms. They do not distinguish between the un-Christian scandal that offends Christ and the holy scandal that is indissolubly linked to Christ.

Because these Catholics have adopted the norms of the enemies of the Church, because they see themselves through the eyes of those who hate the Church, they have a bad conscience. They therefore want to "reform" the Church so that it will be acceptable by the standards of its enemies. They often consider this attitude a sign of open-mindedness, of unprejudiced objectivity. But this is a great self-delusion. In reality, they are interpreting their religious insecurity, the weakness of their faith in the divine revelation entrusted to the Church, and the attraction of worldly norms as a virtue, when it is only evidence of human frailty. This fear of the world, of public opinion, is the same attitude one could observe in National Socialist Germany. Many whom one would never have expected to yield to the Nazi ideology were gradually infected by it—even some theologians.

But the greatest source of secularist infiltration of the Church today is to be found in those progressives who have actually lost their faith and instead of leaving the Church have decided to "reform" it. They are in love with the spirit of the world; they care more for the alleged progress of civilization than for the eternal welfare of individual persons, or the glorification of God. Here, the process of secularization reaches its climax. This is no longer a mistaken apologetic which leads people to accept the false norms of the world. It is more than a vulnerability to criticism based on a false scale of values. It is a total adherence to these false, worldly norms. It regards the Church as a mere human institution (which does not have an infallible magisterium), subject to an historical evolution in which one "truth" can be replaced by another. This position declares that the Church does not possess absolute truth, but only strives to reach it gradually. Under the guise of propagating a Christianity that suits modern man, this "reform" is an utter betrayal of Christ.

Maritain has rightly said that the present crisis in the Church is the worst in history because today the heretics remain in the Church. But although this strange fact is especially disturbing, it should not discourage us: we must never forget that Judas Iscariot was not an outsider.

XVII

The Unchanging Value
of Contemplation

From the fatuous myth of the "modern man" there evolves
the notion of adapting Christian revelation and the Christian
concept of the meaning and end of man's life to the spirit of
our present epoch. Its absurdity becomes strikingly apparent
when some "progressive Catholics" speak about religious
orders and especially about contemplative orders. They who
believe that the meaning and value of a contemplative life,
the vocation to it, and the calling to concentrate totally on
God, depend upon the circumstances of an historical epoch
or—still worse—upon the "mentality" of an epoch instead
of upon the call addressed by God to the individual soul,
betray themselves as being ignorant of the supernatural.

There have obviously been religious orders founded at
special times for special purposes. The Trinitarians' aim, for
instance, was the liberation of Christians who had fallen into
the hands of the Arabs or the Turks; and, of course, such
religious orders may lose their *raison d'être* because of
changes in the course of history. But the belief that the very
soul and meaning of religious life and of contemplation can
become obsolete in the course of history simply shows that

one has eliminated the supernatural. Even a "progressive Catholic" would call it sheer nonsense to say that murder and theft could suddenly change in their immorality because we now live in 1968 instead of 1550. But one hears too often that what was all right in the religious sphere four hundred years ago cannot be valid for today. This notion fails to reckon with supernatural reality; it comes of looking at these things as if there had never been a Christian revelation. If holiness is no longer the end for Christians, if transformation in Christ, the *imitatio Christi*, is replaced by serving the world, by being a useful member of the State or of any natural society, or by self-fulfillment, then obviously monasteries no longer have any sense whatever and the evangelical counsels would have been wrong advice.

One cannot expect a militant atheist to have any understanding of the value, meaning and *raison d'être* of contemplative religious orders. He will consistently plead for an abolition of monasteries. But "progressives" do not openly come to this conclusion. Instead of flatly denying the supernatural, they put it in brackets. They advocate a "reform" amounting to a change of the ideals and aims of religious life—indeed, to a contradiction of the very meaning of that life. All religious orders—and especially all contemplative orders—become ludicrous if we leave supernatural reality out of the account; if we pay no attention to the words of Christ: "Mary has chosen the better part"; if we deny or overlook the character of our earthly life as a pilgrimage.

Criticism of the present state of contemplative monasteries and suggestions of reform can make sense and can claim competence only if we keep in mind the very meaning of these monasteries. And this implies that we believe fully in the reality of the supernatural, that we recognize that earthly life has the character of a *status viae*. It implies the belief that the very meaning and end of our life is to glorify God, and to become transformed in Christ. If, on the contrary, we hold that this belief and this conception of our life have changed because man has allegedly come of age, then any criticism, any suggestion concerning contemplative monasteries—or, for that matter, concerning any monasteries—has no meaning and no interest whatever. "Reformers" who have forgotten what it was all about are clearly incompetent. It is as if a ferocious misogynist, a man who has never loved and considers love to be a lunatic intoxication, proposes to reform marriage. Having lost the *sensus supranaturalis*, these "Catholics" could take only one consistent position, namely the abolition of all monasteries and religious orders. This position would at least be sincere and not self-contradictory.

Through, With, and In Christ

Contemplation has fundamental, irreplaceable value for any true Christian whether he lives in the world or is a member of a religious order. Certainly, monasteries whose sole end is contemplation presuppose a specific vocation—but it is a glorious, sublime vocation. This can be understood only if one grasps the unique function of such a life in the Mystical Body of Christ, if one believes in a purely supernatural fruitfulness instead of restricting fruitfulness to a visible, tangible efficacy. The key to contemplation either within or outside of religious orders is the belief that only through Christ, with Christ and in Christ are we able to glorify God, to become saints, to love our neighbor, to help him on his way to God, to enrich the Mystical Body of Christ. All this depends exclusively on our relationship to Jesus Christ, the God-man. The degree of our communion with Jesus, its depth, its primacy in our lives, determines the degree of our "usefulness" in the vineyard of the Lord. Only in our direct concentration on Christ, in our personal love of

Jesus, can our souls be fecundated in such a way that the supernatural life, which we received in Baptism, can fully unfold itself and bear fruit. In this direct confrontation with Christ all natural gifts can be transfigured and completely new forces, new powers and new virtues be granted to us. From this alone emerges the victorious, liberating influence on others, a radiance into the world, which we witness in all the saints.

Mediocrity in Contemplative Life Is Fatal

This certainly does not require contemplation to play the same role for lives in the world as it does in contemplative orders. But it sheds light on the sublimity of such a vocation and on its fruitfulness. This vocation implies an enormous spiritual thirst, a unique awakeness, a deep longing for union with Christ. Let us not forget that the founders of these orders were saints and mystics. The higher a vocation ranks (and the more that is required to live up to it), the more it becomes vulnerable to being turned into something negative—into a caricature of itself. This applies even to certain higher professions in the natural order. Nothing is worse than a philosopher who has neither real thirst and zeal for truth, nor the intellectual and moral equipment needed to find it. His "work" is either a waste of time or a grave nuisance. The same applies to all artists, whereas the accomplishments of a laborer, an employee, a schoolteacher can still have a certain value even if the person is only modestly gifted. Thus, it is no wonder that for such a high vocation as the contemplative one, mediocrity is especially fatal. It greatly endangers the worth of this vocation. Such perversions as day-dreaming and sentimental illusions deprive such a life of its value. But is this not the drawback of all great and outstanding things, that they imply a risk and that not living

152

up to them becomes worse than "to tread the path of gener-ality" (to use Kierkegaard's expression)? "If I have rarely found better Christians than those who have lived rightly in monasteries, I can also say that I have never seen worse ones than those who have gone astray in them. But if we are saddened by so much defilement, let us be consoled by the spectacle of so much goodness" (St. Augustine, Letter 78.8).

To Glorify God—the Work of Saints

The meaning of a cloistered Carmelite monastery comes forth clearly when we think of the many saints and saintly souls that this order has offered to God and offered for the Church, beginning with St. Teresa of Avila, to St. Thérèse of Lisieux, to Elizabeth of the Trinity. A single one of these saints or saintly souls justifies the existence of this order because one of these souls glorified God more than innumer-able mediocre Christians (efficient as these may be in other respects), and is a greater gift for the world than these. But even all those religious who do not achieve this highest goal, but who strive for it with a sincere and firm will, glorify God and bear witness to the sublime character and value of this order. Certainly the superior should be careful and severe in the acceptance of nuns in a Carmelite monastery and exam-ine thoroughly whether they have the very special vocation needed for it. There is an inherent danger in human nature from which religious orders are not exempt, namely, to aim at a numerical growth—to consider the number of members in the order as a gain. It is a deeply human, natural tendency, which is to be found in all worldly organizations such as political parties and civic associations. In these latter cases numerical growth is a great help to attain a practical end, but when this tendency creeps into monasteries, especially into monasteries of a most severe character, it becomes a great danger. Here there is no practical end that depends upon the size of the community. Here the only ends are the glorification of God, the sanctification of the individual and the building of a holy community. Growth is no advantage, but a nuisance, if by growth is meant accepting members who do not have a full vocation. Certainly one can rejoice when more people have a real and genuine thirst for this heroic life, but the joy is then motivated by the fact that so many individual souls have been filled with this holy fire and by this zeal for glorifying God. However, every soul who enters without this true vocation is a burden for the order, and an unhappiness to himself. The desire that the community grow should never influence the superiors in such a way as to prevent them from severely testing whether or not a real vocation is given in each case.

We can, moreover, never understand the meaning of such a monastery if we are blind to the supernatural fruitfulness of the Carmelite life. We should not speak about "reform" of contemplative monasteries, if we no longer believe that the sacrifices and prayers have a deep and great influence on innumerable souls outside the monastery—on the entire Church and world. We are not qualified to reform an order if we no longer believe in this supernatural mystery to which so many events in the history of the Church, and in the lives of saints, clearly bear witness.

Certainly nothing is safe from abuses. If abuses were an argument against the thing which is abused, democracy would have to be considered a great evil because it certainly is very often abused. And what about abuses against such a high good as marriage? After all, many marriages are contracted for the sake of money or for other superficial reasons. There are many adulteries committed. Would this justify the claim that marriage should be replaced by something else? We do not reform anything by actually scrapping it.

There is also no human guarantee that real perversions (which must be clearly distinguished from abuses) will not enter the sanctuary of a contemplative monastery. No rule can prevent the spirit of laxity, self-indulgence, narrowness, mediocrity or pettiness from creeping in—or the failure to distinguish the essential from the non-essential, the spirit from the letter. There is and forever will be but one remedy against these perversions and imperfections: that the superior and every member go back to the authentic spirit of the order, that they renew again and again their striving to be transformed in Christ, to cooperate with His grace. This will fill the atmosphere of the monastery with supernatural glory, and generate supernatural influence well beyond its walls.

It is, by the way, most peculiar that those who want to adapt religious life to the mentality of our epoch have so little perception of the deeper yearning of men of this age, of any age. Contrary to their vociferous claim, they simply do not have their ear to the ground. Contemplation was and remains a primeval longing of mankind. (There is perhaps an indication of this, though dreadfully perverted, in the modern fad of Oriental ways of meditation.)

The sublime value of authentically contemplative monasteries does not vanish with time; neither does the important role of contemplation for reaching the real meaning of our lives in the world—to be transformed in Christ.

"I cannot become transformed in Thee unless that holy stillness spread out in me; unless Thy gifts of grace and the calls of Thy love slowly expand and mature in my soul. Therefore, wherever Thy will has placed me, it will always be my chief task to face Thee, free from all haste of earthly activities; to drink in Thy love, and to live in Thee, loving and adoring" (Von Hildebrand, *Transformation in Christ*, p. 120).

XVIII

The Dutch Bishops

[Less than a year after the close of the Second Vatican Council, the Sacred Congregation for the Doctrine of the Faith identified ten errors of doctrine as being of special concern, and asked all the bishops to report on their prevalence. The second and fourth themes mentioned by the Congregation drew a response from the Dutch bishops that was remarkable for its arrogance and slovenliness, even in the generally prideful and sloppy '60s. Much of von Hildebrand's analysis of the Dutch effort is of timeless value as an assertion of the immutability of truth and of plain standards of intellectual honesty.—Ed.]

Theme II. Formulation of Dogma: It is said that dogmatic formulations are to be subject to historical evolution to the extent that even their objective meaning is subject to change.

Theme IV. Truth: Some virtually deny absolute, firm and immutable objective truth, and subject everything to a certain relativism, and this indeed with that counterfeit reasoning according to which all truth inevitably follows a rhythm of evolution and history.

The Dutch bishops' answer is perhaps the most noteworthy of any of the known responses to the letter of the Holy

See because, while denying that the errors have appeared in Holland, it unintentionally confirms that they are spreading among some theologians and even in segments of the Dutch hierarchy itself. One could hardly think of a better proof of the existence of these errors than the answer of the Dutch bishops; the errors are present in the very content of their reply.

Much of the reply sounds deeply religious, but it is at bottom specious and meaningless; sophisms blur the real issue; clever-sounding arguments turn out to be untenable under scrutiny. No embellishments can conceal the fact that this very answer of the Dutch bishops is itself incompatible with authentic Catholic teaching and Christian revelation.

The Dutch bishops speak of new "discoveries" in the doctrines of the Church, but the contributions to theology by great, deep minds of the past, Fathers of the Church, saints and mystics, do not have the character of "discoveries." They are luminous elaborations of revealed truth or refutations of heresies, based solely on the truth entrusted to the infallible magisterium of the Church. It is quite clear that the "new discoveries" (the term betrays the influence of Heideggerianism), which they say should be integrated, are either fashionable philosophies or pseudo-scientific contrivances.

The bishops say we must *aim* at truth; but striving for it would be a meaningless process—a work of Sisyphus—if we did not possess certain absolute truths which are presupposed for all exploration—for instance, the laws of logic. Moreover, how can we know that there is an absolute, objective truth? Does the statement that there is an absolute truth which we do not possess but can only aim at not itself present itself as an absolute truth which we possess? This is truly nothing but old, full-fledged relativism.

The possibility of transcending my own mind and possessing certainty about the existence and nature of certain beings is the very basis for the most decisive and characteristic experiences of a person.

Why do the bishops claim, for example, that the "meaning" (signification) of Christ is primarily our salvation? It is obviously a complete abuse of the term "meaning" when one restricts it to the effect on us. But above all, our redemption, our salvation, stands and falls with the objective reality of Christ's divinity.

This distinction of being and meaning stems from Heidegger. It is based on a wrong and muddled metaphysics; it is not an adequate excuse for the trotting out of old heresies.

The Divinity of Christ

Time and again heresies have arisen that have denied the divinity of Christ and time and again the councils have condemned them. It is the central question of the Christian faith. It was a scandal for the Jews and foolishness for the Greeks. It will always remain an inscrutable mystery—neither easier nor more difficult to believe now than it was two thousand years ago.

But if a full and univocal profession of the divinity of Christ is withheld, the very core and ground of Christian faith, of Christianity, Christendom and the Church, vanishes.

The Dutch bishops evade this central issue. In fact, they even advance the possibility that Christ had a human father, saying it is "not entirely decided" whether or not Joseph was the progenitor, and that perhaps Mary was only "figuratively" a virgin. Instead of a clear and unambiguous profession, we find complicated and obscure meddling: "Christ is the *son* of God insofar as he offers the salvation which *God* grants to man, and *man* because he offers it to man." If we compare this with the Creed of Nicaea: "*Et in unum Dominum Jesum Christum, filium Dei unigenitum,....Deum de Deo, lumen de lumine, Deum verum de Deo vero,"* we cannot but see the tendency to replace clear facts, which nevertheless are an unfathomable mystery, by tortured and ambiguous speculations which, for the gullible public, evoke the impression of depth, but in reality consist of empty words.

The bishops say that the Church must offer a new interpretation of the divinity of Christ, because it has, they claim, become more difficult than it was in former times for "modern man" to accept that Christ is the son of God. This claim is pregnant with completely arbitrary, unproven and even patently wrong assumptions. Neither is it more difficult to believe in the divinity of Christ now than it was in other times, nor is it true that laypeople have addressed a petition for a new interpretation. The decline of faith, the crisis in the Church, started among the clergy. They say that the new presentation is dictated by pastoral concerns and flows out of charity for the faithful. This is a mere euphemism, to say the least.

How can such a pollution of doctrine as there is here be considered helpful to the faithful?

An Immanentist Tendency

A disastrous immanentism and pragmatism disclose themselves when the authors assert that it is good and Christian that under the influence of Bultmann and existentialist thought (and stemming from Heidegger) emphasis is laid on the offer of salvation, even though the Redeemer Himself is placed more in the background. In reality salvation, as well as all our faith and hope, rest on the reality of the God-man, Christ. In subordinating the *truth* of revelation to its effect on our souls, we necessarily undermine that very effect. They introduce a difference between the "being" and "meaning" of Christ and stress the importance of the "meaning" (signification). The "distinction" is very muddled. The ineffable holiness of Christ's sacred humanity, the epiphany of God in Him, the fact that it is the Second Person of the Trinity Who assumed human nature—all this belongs to His Being. That He is Our Redeemer, that on the Cross He expiated the sins of the world, that He is the Lamb of God Who takes away the sins of the world, all this likewise belongs to His Being. The Being of the God-man includes infinite plenitude of "meaning." Why claim that the "meaning" of Christ is primarily our salvation? It is obviously an abuse of the term "meaning" when one restricts it to the effect on us. But above all, our redemption, our salvation, stands or falls with the objective reality of Christ's divinity. An immanentist and pragmatist tendency leads to the illusion that it would be possible to save the effect of the "good tidings" or to retain the joy and hope in the soul of the faithful, if the Church were no longer able to affirm univocally the divinity of Christ and His resurrection. The shelteredness in Christ's redemption would become nothing but an unwarranted optimism and illusion, if the content of faith were replaced by equivocal, murky speculation.

This distinction of being and meaning (signification) stems from Heidegger. It is based on his unfounded theory that the human person, who alone is a *"Dasein,"* according to him, endows the *"Seiendes"* (the impersonal world) with meaning, implying that this *"Seiendes"* is chaotic until man has given structure and form to it. And these ambiguous, doubtful speculations are taken for granted. Indeed, they are thought to be a symptom of "having come of age"!

The same hazy thinking is manifested when the authors deal with the resurrection of Christ. When they say that the resurrection of Christ is not an object of factual substantiation but of faith, the public may have the impression that the mystery of Christ's resurrection is being enhanced, but in reality there is here the same noncommittal attitude which was shown towards the divinity of Christ. The distinction here between factual substantiation and faith is completely misleading. It serves only to avoid a clear profession of the fact of Christ's resurrection.

Facts and Mysteries

In the frame of the deposit of Catholic faith there are firstly *facts*, which have been seen and testified to by the Apostles; secondly, there are mysteries which we believe because Christ has told them to the Apostles. The sacred humanity of Christ, which could never be invented by a human mind, His ineffable holiness—revealed in every deed and word spoken by Him—have been seen and *grasped* by the Apostles. "We have been eyewitnesses of His exaltation" (II Peter 1:16). His miracles and, above all, His resurrection have been reported as facts with evidence by the Apostles. They bore witness to this. ("We saw His glory," says St. John 1:14.) All this is the basis of our faith in Christ. On the other hand, the mysteries of the Incarnation, of the Trinity and of the Real Presence of Christ in the Eucharist, are not objects of factual substantiation, but of faith. They are deep mysteries; they are to be believed, accepted on the authority of Christ and His holy Church. Thus it is an equivocal statement to say of the resurrection of Christ that it is not an object of factual substantiation but an object of faith.

That their objective reality can be accepted with absolute certainty applies as much to the mysteries of faith, which we accept on the authority of the word of Christ and His Church, as it applies to the facts which the Apostles have seen, albeit these facts are, themselves, unfathomable and mysterious. If our Faith were not based on facts that have been testified to by witnesses, it would be suspended in mid-air, so to speak.

The testimony of the Apostles is the foundation. Upon this factual witness do we believe in Christ; upon it we have confidence and faith in Him and in His words. Not only do the Gospels testify to these facts, the Act of the Apostles, the words of St. Peter and the epistles of St. Paul, all speak of eyewitnesses of Christ's resurrection.

The declaration that the resurrection is an object of faith and not of factual substantiation, is nothing but an attempt to put its objective reality into parentheses. This comes clearly to the fore, in the introductory words which declare that doubt or hesitant formulations concerning the resurrection or His existence as the risen Christ are the results of a new exegesis of the last chapters of the Gospels, or the "insight" that the resurrection of Jesus is no object for a statement of facts. Once again the very doubtful pseudoscientific guessing of the professors of exegesis is made a norm for the doctrine of the Church.

Cardinal Newman says:

> And so again, when a man has become a Catholic, were he to set about following a doubt which has occurred to him, he has already disbelieved....No; Scripture did not make them disbelieve (impossible!); they disbelieved *when* they opened the Bible; they opened it in an unbelieving spirit, and for an unbelieving purpose; they would not have opened it, had they not anticipated—I might say, hoped—that they should find things there inconsistent with Catholic teaching. They begin in self-will and disobedience, and they end in apostasy.—(*Discourses to Mixed Congregations*, Discourse XI, "Faith And Doubt.")

And the authors propound the *insight* that Christ's resurrection is not an object for a statement of facts but for faith, and they adduce I Cor. 15, 42-49 in support of their theory. But there St. Paul speaks of the general resurrection of the flesh. And with all their "scientific" criticism they seem to forget, or at least do not include, the words said about the historical, objective fact of the resurrection of Christ at the beginning of that very chapter (I Cor. 15): "The chief message I handed on to you, as it was handed to me, was that He...rose again on the third day...that He was seen by Cephas, then by the eleven Apostles, and afterwards by more than five hundred of the brethren at once, most of whom are still alive today." *Insight*? Who had this insight? What kind of insight is this? The specific field of insights is philosophy.

The so-called insight is introduced as indubitable—and the relativism professed earlier is suddenly dropped. Is the modest and cautious attitude (praised at first by the authors), the critical sense of the modern man, not suddenly replaced by an unwarranted dogmatic absolutism—in calling "insight" what is in reality a twisted theory of some professors of theology, who have succumbed to the influence of fashionable and false philosophies?

A Refutation of Certain Opinions

It may be well here to refute some of these different opinions of the new exegetes concerning Christ's resurrection. All of them point in the direction of there being no factual substantiation for it.

It is true that, according to the Scriptures, Christ's actual rising out of the tomb was not witnessed; but the fact that the tomb was empty is clearly testified to.

Did the disciples take the body out of the tomb? Such a removal would have been a very difficult thing. The rock closing the tomb was of a remarkable size, as is stated in the Gospel. It is very improbable, to say the least, that the disciples could have rolled aside such a stone and made off with the body unnoticed by the guards whose sole duty was to prevent any such thing. Even if the guards had all fallen asleep, such activity would have awakened them.

The fact that the risen Christ was not seen by all men, but only by the Apostles and holy women, in no way indicates that He did not really rise, nor does it indicate that the Apostles only saw Him because they believed He had risen. In reality they did not expect His resurrection—although it had been predicted—and were, in fact, deeply mourning His death. The fact that He was not immediately recognized by the disciples in Emmaus is rather an argument against the thesis that they only had a vision of Him. They spoke with a real person and suddenly recognized that this real person was Christ. Why should He not choose to make Himself unrecognizable in this specific case? And when He appeared to the Apostles, with only St. Thomas missing, He was seen by them, ate with them, spoke to them and said most important things. Can this be historically explained as a mere common faith and act of belief, instead of an overwhelming experience? They saw and grasped something that changed their entire mood. And their surprise was great when confronted with this clear fact. So much so that at first they could not believe:

"The Apostles did not believe Mary Magdalen, nor the two disciples who had walked with Him" (Mark 16:12-13). "But to their minds the story seemed madness, and they could not believe it" (Luke 24:2).

But then Christ stood in their midst, and in His mercy established it as a fact beyond a doubt that He had truly risen, by saying:

'Touch me and look; a spirit has not flesh and bones as you see that I have.' And as He spoke thus, He showed

them His hands and feet. Then, while they were still
doubtful and bewildered with joy, He asked them: 'Have
you anything to eat?' (Luke 24:39-41)

When they spoke to St. Thomas about it, he would not
accept it. He was just as much a believer in Christ as the other
Apostles, but he had not expected His resurrection any more
than they had. St. Thomas was, in fact, most sober and
reasonable. His skeptical attitude was certainly not com-
mendable, but it does definitely demolish any thesis that the
Apostles were carried away by some sort of intoxication of
belief in Christ, some sort of marvelous state of mind which
made them have visions of Him; or that it was only in their
faith that they saw the risen Christ, or that the resurrected
was the object of their faith alone. No. St. Thomas really made
a factual substantiation of Christ's resurrection. Only when
he had established this as a fact, and it was a most surprising,
incredible fact (incredible because miraculous), only when
he had substantiated it in an even more concrete way than
the other Apostles, in touching the wounds, did he believe.

For something had taken place which was incredible; *yet,
it had taken place.* They were brought to believe not alone
through their eyes, but through their hands, so that faith
might enter their heart by way of their senses, so that the
faith thus entering their hearts might be preached
throughout the world.—St. Augustine (PL 38, *Col* 657,
Sermo 116) (Emphasis added.)

Then follow the many proofs on which would rest the
authority of the faith that was to be preached to the whole
world. These proofs recounted in the Gospels abun-
dantly established the reality of the Lord's resurrection....—St. Leo (PL 54, *Sermo* 71)

The whole historical life of Christ is filled with miraculous deeds. Why should He not disclose His Risen Self only to those to whom He had entrusted divine revelation? To conclude from this that this resurrection is no historical fact is absolutely unscientific and illogical.

Arbitrary Definitions of Fact

Some exegetes set up an arbitrary definition of the notion of historical fact. But what matters is not the question of whether or not Christ's resurrection was an historical fact in this arbitrary sense of the word, but the simple question whether it really objectively took place as did any other true event of history, or whether it was only something accepted by the Apostles without any basis in fact.

It would make sense to say that Christ's resurrection is an object of faith only if one wanted thereby to express the idea that the Apostles believed in it exclusively because Christ had predicted before His death that He would rise on the third day—in the same way as they believed in eternal life or in the existence of Hell exclusively because He had repeatedly spoken of them. However, the assumption that the resurrection of Christ was only accepted in faith by the Apostles is clearly contradicted by the Gospels. This was no imagination or hallucination of the Apostles, nor a psychological effect of their strong "faith" and their ardent hope.

It is obvious that this entire argumentation is based on the refusal to accept the possibility of a miracle, the refusal to accept as historical fact anything that cannot be explained by natural causes. Such skepticism makes it necessary to interpret every fact that has the character of a miracle as "not historical." This is nothing but Bultmann's demythologization, which fails to make a distinction between "mythology" and miracles. It also shows an unscientific prejudice.

This foolishness reminds me of what a German historian said concerning the miracles of St. Bernard: "The miracles of St. Bernard have no doubt been recorded in a most reliable way, so that they are unassailable from a historical point of view. One cannot have better historical evidence than this, but obviously they cannot be true because miracles do not exist." Such a conclusion is certainly not scientific and historical; it is based exclusively on false and atheistic philosophical assumptions. It is naive self-delusion to think that an interpretation of Christ's resurrection as a mere object of faith is the result of more advanced "scientific" exegesis. It is nothing but the exhuming of the same old rationalism with all its prejudices.

We see similarly untidy thinking in the thesis that Christ's resurrection is supratemporal, unearthly and so on, and therefore "not a historical fact." These are idle words which blur the facts, and indicate a loss of faith. Instead of clearly denying it as former rationalists did, they circumlocute it, dodge it, hoping thereby to make it "plausible" (as they openly say) for "modern man." These interpretations and this pseudoscientific exegesis are truly time-bound, determined by modish, but totally unproven and even self-contradictory philosophies.

XIX

Living Down to Your Convictions

Father Hans Küng claimed in a speech given at the Vatican Council, and has since repeated the theme frequently, that we live in an epoch characterized by intellectual and moral honesty. I think that Fr. Küng expresses an illusion which is widespread today.

There are many who believe that our present approach to life is more honest, more "genuine," than that of the Victorian era with all its hypocrisy, conventionalism and prudery. No longer does public opinion condemn things that most people have always done clandestinely anyway! No longer do we feel obliged to lie by exhibiting a polite and friendly demeanor when in truth we feel nothing resembling friendliness. No longer are our lives thrust into rigid, artificial forms. Modern man does not feel obliged to cling to traditional opinions; he speaks his personal opinions in full "sincerity." Even when a traditional idea or teaching is beautiful and gladdening to the soul, he still wants to be "realistic" about it, to be free from comforting myths. He wants to face reality *as it is*. The predominance of science in our society is often taken as a decisive proof of intellectual honesty.

This judgment about the alleged virtue of our age betrays, I repeat, a grave illusion: If we analyze it closely, we shall see that what appears to be honesty is, in reality, a sham honesty.

First of all, it is quite wrong to believe that every person who does not live up to his moral ideals is dishonest, or, to put it differently, that consistent agreement between one's principles and one's conduct is the criterion for honesty. It is certainly desirable that a man should live up to his moral convictions (provided the convictions correspond with truth).

But the frequent discrepancy between a man's conduct and his convictions, far from being evidence of dishonesty, is a tragedy rooted in our fallen nature. This classic conflict between deeds and convictions is expressed by Ovid: *Video meliora proboque; deteriora sequor.* St. Paul makes the same point: "For the good which I will I do not: but the evil which I will not, that I do."

To be sure, if a man does not intend to do what he recognizes to be right, if he is indifferent to the problem of making action correspond with principle—if he does what he knows to be wrong without having a burdened conscience—then, morally, he is a very poor person indeed. But to call him *dishonest* is an understatement. His conduct is worse than dishonesty, it betrays either a cynical wickedness or a brutish unscrupulousness. Similarly, the man who strives to live up to what he recognizes to be morally good is in no way dishonest when he does not succeed. On the contrary, it is a specific sign of the man's honesty when he admits that moral laws and moral values are fully valid even though he fails to live up to them. What is dishonest—what is all too characteristic of our age—is for a man to adapt the truth to his actions: to take his *de facto* conduct as the norm, to deny the validity of moral laws because he has not succeeded in living up to them.

In a word, before we can take as a sign of honesty the formal agreement between a man's moral convictions and his conduct, we must ask whether the agreement is the result of living up to his convictions, or of adapting his convictions to his actions.

Living Up to Taboos

Yet even in the former case, we cannot conclude that the man is acting correctly without asking the further question of whether his convictions about morality are true or false, good or evil. In many instances men who have shallow, relativistic theories concerning morality manage to give the morally right responses in their immediate existential contact with reality. The man who holds, as a matter of theory, that moral good and evil are mere taboos may, nevertheless, shrink from committing a cruelty or injustice because (his theories aside) he is aware of the ultimate reality of moral values. Indeed, men are usually more intelligent and closer to truth in their immediate contact with life than in their theoretical reasonings about it. In such cases, agreement between action and theoretical conviction is hardly to be recommended. Rather, to forget these shallow rationalizations is the right thing to do. Here an inconsistency between conviction and action can be a positive good.

It is also a great error to believe that the man who has become morally blind, and proceeds to openly immoral action, is more honest than the one who seeks to hide his immorality from others. It was certainly deplorable when men hid their immoral deeds only out of fear of public opinion. But can the same be said of men who hide their immorality in order to avoid giving a bad example to others, and to avoid giving scandal to the truths which they believe, but which their actions belie?

171

The Victorian Prototype

Let us take the case, however, of the Victorian proto-
type—the hypocrite who tried to hide his immorality out of
self-interest. Was he really worse than the modern man who
sees nothing wrong, for example, with sexual promiscuity
and speaks of it shamelessly? Was the Victorian less honest?
There are two points to be made here. For his part the
Victorian betrayed, by his very hypocrisy, an indirect respect
for moral values. This, of course, the shameless sinner does
not do. But neither does the unapologetic sinner deserve
praise for "honesty." There is no reason, after all, to hide his
moral deviations since he no longer sees anything shocking
in them. Moreover, he has nothing to fear from public opinion, since it has now become fashionable not to be shocked
by promiscuity. What once entitled the Bohemian to regard
himself as a revolutionary—the fact that he fearlessly
shocked public opinion—has today disappeared. It is therefore difficult to understand why anyone today should praise
shamelessness as courageous and honest.

There is a genuine honesty, however, which is truly antithetical to genuine dishonesty. The latter is perfectly exemplified in a Tartuffe—the rascal sanctimoniously acting out
the role of a virtuous person; the intention to attract and cheat
others by apparent virtue is really a peak of dishonesty. Now
the genuine antithetical honesty here is not to be found in the
shameless sinner who makes no attempt to conceal his immorality, but in the virtuous man who out of humility hides
his virtues.

Another false conception of honesty is widespread today—the notion that our exterior behavior should be in full
agreement with our inner feelings and moods. A man is
regarded as dishonest, for instance, if he uses expressions of
politeness that do not correspond with his actual attitude. To
be sure, we could rightly speak of a certain dishonesty—

though disingenuousness would be the better word—when a man behaves as if he were deeply moved, or overjoyed, or indignant, while in reality he experiences nothing of the kind. On the other hand, it is completely wrong to make our feelings the measure of our behavior toward other persons. Rather, our expressions ought to conform to what our attitude *should be*. Whatever our actual feelings toward others, we should be polite and attentive toward them. This is in no way dishonest—any more than it is evidence of "honesty" to behave in an unfriendly, unattentive manner toward someone we do not care for.

This false conception of honesty makes an ideal of self-indulgence, of letting oneself go. It precludes, indeed repudiates, the enrichment of life that observance of adequate forms makes possible. It misses completely the deep meaning, the great educational value, of such forms. Precisely what makes the well-mannered man the superior man is discounted as a mark of dishonesty or insincerity. If this conception of honesty were valid, the ideal "honest man" would necessarily be uncouth, freed of all restraints and self-control. Regression toward Neanderthal man would be the goal desired. Here indeed is a radical reactionary tendency which, significantly, is most prevalent today among self-styled progressives.

The sham character of this conception of honesty is especially evident in the matter of man's relation to God. How often we have heard it said: Why should I pray the *Confiteor* when I do not feel contrite? Why should I accuse myself of sins when I feel quite innocent? How can I pray *De Profundis clamavi ad Te, Domine* when I feel quite jolly? And so on.

The Reality Beyond Moods

The first answer is that my prayers to God should conform to objective reality, not to my accidental mood. I know that I am, in reality, sinful. I know, consequently, that I should feel contrition. This objective reality is the measure of the wording of my prayers to God. The point here is that my prayers should conform with the real situation of man confronting God, and therefore with what I *should* experience in such a confrontation. Here the choice of my words should not be dependent on what I have been permitted to experience. I speak them meaningfully because they correspond to my true situation, to what I ought to experience: the words are the objectification of attitudes which should form me, and into which I want to grow. Not honesty, therefore, but the depths of dishonesty are revealed in the man who, misunderstanding the very purpose and meaning of prayer (or of any cultic act for that matter), refuses to utter words that do not reflect his actual mood. To take one's accidental mood as the only valid norm simply betrays a ridiculous self-centeredness and conceit.

But the error here goes much further still. In liturgical prayer we participate in the prayer of Christ and of His Church. It is, therefore, a community prayer: in any liturgical prayer, I speak out of a spirit of communion with all brethren. Hence, even if my own soul is filled with joy at a given moment I pray with the awareness that many other persons are suffering, that many are mourning: I know that the earth is a valley of tears. I consequently have full reason to pray the *De profundis* even if I happen to feel only grateful joy for a great gift, or to pray a psalm of praise and gratitude when I happen to be undergoing a great trial. It is quite astonishing that this profound community aspect of liturgical prayer should escape notice by some of the very persons who prefer liturgical prayer to private prayer on the grounds that the latter does not further communion among men.

In the intellectual domain also our epoch can hardly be praised for its honesty.

If we think of the way in which religion was attacked by Voltaire or Renan, flat and abominable though their mentality was, it is clear that the old method of attacking religion was more honest than that of many modern thinkers. The latter approach religion, on the surface, in a much more friendly way, but by giving new "interpretations" to Christian truth, and by blurring the difference between authentic revelation and myth, they misrepresent and thus insidiously undermine the very essence of the Christian faith. Formerly, there was an open denial of objective truth on the part of skeptics and radical relativists; today there is an historical relativism that is a more refined and distinguished manner of dissolving truth. It does not openly deny objective truth, but it ends in the same wasteland of skepticism—hardly evidence of intellectual honesty.

Moreover, there is a fashionable method of proceeding in philosophy that seeks to create the impression of depth by an overcomplicated wording which frequently is a cloak for meaninglessness. Employing many self-invented terms, it allegedly solves classical problems by declaring that the problems are stupidly posed, or do not exist, or are unimportant. Is this a sign of intellectual honesty? In comparing several modern philosophers with Plato, Aristotle, St. Augustine, St. Thomas and Descartes, we cannot but admit that our intellectual climate is incomparably less honest than that in which these great thinkers lived.

Freudian Witch Doctors

Other widespread trends of our time betray the same lack of candor, but for a somewhat more complicated reason. We think, for example, of the positivist mentality in its different brands, all of which judge the reality of a being to be in inverse proportion to its metaphysical rank. We think of the

Freudians who claim to be "realistic" in trying to reduce every spiritual, meaningful entity to something not spiritual and not meaningful; who try to convince us that most intellectual processes can be reduced to associations, that love is in reality nothing but sex, that moral values are in reality nothing but superstition, and so on. The disillusion they propose to instill in the "unrealistic" man—i.e., the man not yet exposed to their doctrine—is the path that is supposed to lead to intellectual honesty. Thus they feel very honest indeed as they declare only the lower part of the universe to be real; as they reduce all spiritual relations and all motivations to mechanical processes; as they strip the universe of all meaningful content; as they debunk all objective values. Have they not freed others from their illusions? Have they not presented a realistic version of the world?

It remains to ask whether their conception of the universe is true. If their view of the universe is a great error, it makes no sense to praise their "honesty." And the fact is that their view of the universe is a great error. These men are to be credited with spreading superstitions. Their whole doctrine rests on a denial of what experience shows a thing to be, on the claim of being able "to go behind" the thing to discover what it "really is." But is this not exactly what the superstitious man does when he goes "behind" the simple things of experience and professes to read an allegedly "true import"?

If we ponder the psychological sources of this superstition about the universe—this seeing the universe *à la baisse,* this denial of the spiritual universe in the name of a pseudo-realism—it becomes clear that pride and spiritual laziness are at its root. There is a specific obstinacy here, the kind that is exhibited when men seek an entity in a way and direction which, by the very nature of the entity, prohibits them from finding it—the obstinacy of the one who argues with apparently unbiased logic from a planted axiom to a predetermined conclusion. Such men refuse to cooperate with the nature of reality. There is no reason at all for praising as honest an approach obscured by these prejudices. We should remark, rather, the kind of intellectual dishonesty that occurs in every prejudiced type of knowledge.

The man who admits the full reality of the spiritual universe, in a word, is the one who deserves to be praised as honest.

We have already glanced at the absolutely flat, dilettante chatter that has become fashionable among many Catholic lay theologians, unfortunately and irresponsibly appointed to various Catholic colleges. Their insipid discussions about God and the world, their drivel about whether God still fits in our society, whether we still "need" Him, is proof, not only of stupidity, but also of dishonesty. When they deal in the most trivial way with questions of ultimate importance, which have preoccupied and moved men throughout history, and when they argue from points of view that are totally unfitting to the subject, they reveal themselves as exhibitionists and frauds.

Of course in any epoch there are invariably several different and contradictory trends at work, some praiseworthy, some not. The irony, in this case, is that progressive Catholics are today singling out for praise the one trend that is perhaps least deserving of praise.

XX

Teilhard de Chardin: Towards a New Religion

I met Teilhard de Chardin in 1951 at a dinner arranged by Fr. Robert Gannon, S.J., then president of Fordham University. The noted scholars Henri de Lubac and Msgr. Bruno de Solages had highly recommended him. I was therefore full of expectations. After the meal, Fr. Teilhard delivered a long exposition of his views. The lecture was a great disappointment, for it manifested utter philosophical confusion, especially regarding Teilhard's conception of the human person. I was even more upset by his theological primitiveness, because he ignored completely the decisive difference between nature and supernature. After a lively discussion in which I ventured a criticism of his ideas, I had the occasion to speak to Teilhard personally. As our talk touched on St. Augustine, he exclaimed violently: "Don't mention this unfortunate man; he spoiled everything by introducing the supernatural."

This remark confirmed the impression I had gained of the crass naturalism of his views; but it also struck me in another way: the criticism of St. Augustine—the greatest of the Fathers of the Church—betrayed Teilhard's lack of a genuine sense of intellectual and spiritual grandeur.

It was only after reading several of Teilhard's works, however, that I fully realized the catastrophic implications of his philosophical ideas, and the absolute incompatibility of his theology-fiction (as Etienne Gilson calls it) with Christian revelation and the doctrine of the Church.

Many Catholics view Teilhard de Chardin as a great scientist who has reconciled science with the Christian faith by introducing a new theology and metaphysics that take modern scientific findings into account and thus fit into our scientific age. But a reconciliation of science and the Christian faith has never been needed because true science (as distinct from false philosophies disguised in scientific garments) can never be incompatible with Christian faith. Science can neither prove nor disprove the truth of the faith.

Neither are full-time scientists impressed by Teilhard's efforts. "Teilhard is not a biologist," says Jean Rostand, "he has neither the formation nor the knowledge, nor the spirit of a biologist....He deliberately ignores embryology...." Sir Peter Medawar, the Nobel Prize winner, speaks of Teilhard's mental confusion and the exaggerated expression that borders, he says, on hysteria. He says of *The Human Phenomenon* that it is unscientific in its procedure. Sir Peter adds that Teilhard's works in general lack scientific structure, that his competence in his field is modest, that he knows neither what a logical argument is nor what a scientific proof is, that he does not respect the norms which are required for scientific scholarship.

Artful Jumper

I do not know of another thinker who so artfully jumps from one position to another, contradictory one, without noticing the jump or minding it. One is driven therefore to speak of the underlying trend of his thought, to identify the logical consequences of the core of his doctrine—of what was dearest to him.

One of the most striking philosophical shortcomings of Teilhard's system is his conception of man. It is a great irony that the author of *The Human Phenomenon* should completely miss the nature of man as a *person*. He fails to recognize the abyss separating a person from the entire impersonal world around him, and the wholly new dimension of being that a person implies.

Teilhard sees "self-consciousness" as the only difference between men and a highly developed animal. But a comparison of the limited type of consciousness that can be observed in animals with the manifold aspects of a person's consciousness shows instantly how wrong it is to regard the latter as merely an addition of *self-consciousness*. Personal consciousness actualizes itself in knowledge—in the luminous consciousness of an object that reveals itself to our mind, in the capacity to adapt our mind to the nature of the object *(adequatio intellectus ad rem)*, in an understanding of the object's nature. It also actualizes itself in the process of inferring, in the capacity to ask questions, to pursue truth; and in the capacity to build an I-thou communion with another person.

All of this implies a completely new type of consciousness, an entirely new dimension of being. But this marvel of the human mind, which is also revealed in language and in man's role as *homo pictor*, is altogether lost on Teilhard because he insists on viewing human consciousness as merely an *awareness* of self that has gradually developed out of animal consciousness. The scholastics accurately grasped the dimensions of personal consciousness by calling the person a being that *possesses* itself. Compared with the person, every impersonal being sleeps, as it were: it simply endures its existence. Only in the human person do we find an awakened being, a being truly possessing itself, notwithstanding its contingency.

Teilhard's disregard of the person approaches complete inanity when he claims in *The Phenomenon of Man* that a collective consciousness would constitute a higher state of evolution. The idea is of the earth not only becoming covered by countless grains of thought, but becoming enclosed in a single thinking envelope so as to form, functionally, no more than a single vast grain of thought on the sidereal scale.

Here several grave errors are combined. First, the idea of a non-individual consciousness is contradictory. Second, it is wrong to suppose that this impossible fiction could contain something superior to individual personal existence. Third, the idea of a "superconsciousness" is, in fact, a totalitarian ideal: it implies an absolute antithesis to true community, which presupposes essentially individual persons.

Self-Annihilation

The existence of a human person is so essentially individual that the idea of fusing two persons in one is radically impossible. It is also impossible to wish to be another person. We can only wish to be *like* another person. For at the exact moment we should become the other person we would necessarily cease to exist. It belongs to the very nature of the human being, as person, that he remains this one individual being. God could annihilate him, although revelation tells us that this is not God's intention. But to suppose that a human being could give up his individual character without ceasing to exist, without being annihilated by that act, is tantamount to blindness to what a person is.

Some men claim to experience a kind of "union with the cosmos" which "enlarges" their individual existence and presents itself as the acquisition of a superconsciousness. In reality, however, this union exists only in the consciousness of the individual person who has such an experience. Its content—i.e., the feeling of fusion with the cosmos—is in reality the peculiar experience of one concrete person, and in no way implies a collective consciousness.

From what has been said about Teilhard's ideal of the "collective man," it should be clear that he fails to understand, not only the nature of man, as person, but also the nature of true communion and community. For true personal communion (in which a much deeper union is attained than in any ontological fusion) presupposes the favorable individual character of the person. Compared to the union achieved by the conscious interpenetration of souls in mutual love, all fusion of impersonal beings is mere juxtaposition.

Teilhard's ideal of "superhumanity" —his totalitarian conception of community—shows the same naive ignorance of the abyss that separates the glorious realm of personal existence from the impersonal world. It also reveals his blindness to the hierarchy of being and to the hierarchy of values. Pascal "Man is but a reed, the most feeble thing in nature..." But he admirably illuminates the incomparable superiority of one individual person to the entire impersonal world when he added to this famous remark: "but if the universe were to crush him, man would still be more noble than that which killed him; he knows that he dies, and the advantage which the universe has over him, the universe knows nothing of this."

Deceptive Disclaimer

Another aspect of Teilhard's blindness to the essentially individual character of the person is his inordinate interest in man as species. Again he overlooks the differences between humans and mere animals. A dominant interest in the species is quite normal as long as one deals with animals. But it becomes grotesque when human beings are involved. Kierkegaard brought out this point when he stressed the absolute superiority of the individual human being to the human species. Teilhard's own approach is betrayed by his attitude toward the Hiroshima bomb. The alleged progress of humanity which he sees in the invention of nuclear weapons matters more to him than the destruction of innumerable lives and the most terrible sufferings inflicted on individual persons.

It is true that time and again Teilhard speaks of the personal and of the superiority of the personal over the impersonal. Indeed, he often explicitly rejects the possibility that the existence of the individual person will dissolve. He writes, for instance, in *Building the Earth*: "Since there is neither fusion nor dissolution of individual persons the center which they aspire to reach must necessarily be distinct from them, that is, it must have its own personality, its autonomous reality." Yet two pages later we find him rhapsodizing about "the totalization of the individual in the collective man." Teilhard then explains how this contradiction will dissolve in the Omega: "All these so-called impossibilities come about under the influence of love."

It has become fashionable nowadays to accept contradictions as a sign of philosophical depth. They are regarded as antagonistic only as long as the discussion remains on a logical level, and without interest as soon as it reaches the religious sphere. But this fashion does not do away with the essential impossibility of combining contradictions. No amount of modish paradoxes, of emotional effusions, of exotically capitalized words, can conceal Teilhard's fundamental lack of understanding of the nature of the person. The notion of the "personal" in Teilhard's system is stripped of any real meaning by the system's underlying pantheism. "Collective man" and the "totalization" of man represent an ideal that is objectively incompatible with the existence of the individual person—or, rather, necessarily implies the annihilation of the person.

We can understand that his monistic tendency leads him to try to liquidate all real antitheses. He wants to keep the integrity of the person, but he rhapsodizes about totalization. He reduces all contraries to different aspects of one thing, and then claims that the antithetical character of the propositions in question is due merely to an isolation or to an overemphasis of a single aspect. Yet by reading Teilhard closely, one can always detect his primary concern, can always tell where he is going. A passage on the differences between democracy, communism and fascism in *Building the Earth* is illustrative. A superficial reading of the passage could give the impression that Teilhard does not deny the individual character of man. But a closer, critical study against the background of other passages clearly reveals not only an impossible attempt to link together individuality and totalization, but also where Teilhard is aiming, what his main ideal is, where his heart is. It is, once again, with totalization, with superhumanity in the Omega.

The penchant for liquidating antitheses also sheds light on Teilhard's false conception of the community, of the union of persons. It is all conceived upon the pattern of fusion in the realm of matter, and thus misses the radical difference between unification in the sphere of matter and the spiritual union that comes to pass, through real love, in the sphere of individual persons. For Teilhard, love is merely cosmic energy: "...that energy which having generally agitated the cosmic mass, emerges from it to form the Noosphere, what name must be given to such an influence? One only —love." A man who can write that has obviously failed to grasp the nature of this supreme act which by its very essence presupposes a conscious, personal being, and the existence of a Thou. There is no place in the unanimity and harmony of Teilhard's totalitarian communion for a real giving of oneself in love. This unanimity and harmony is actualized through a convergence into one mind, and thus differs radically from the *concordia*, from the blissful union of which the Liturgy of the Mandatum speaks: *"Congregavit nos in unum Christi amor."* The latter is not a "co-thinking," but a mutual, reciprocal love and a unification in Christ based on the personal love response which every individual gives to Christ.

In a monistic world, there is no place for the *intentio unionis*, and the *intentio benevolentiae* proper to real love. For in such a world "cosmic energy" moves everything independently of man's free response. When we interpret things that are merely analogous as constituting an ontological unity, or when we use as literal a term that is metaphysical and analogous, we necessarily bar the way to a real understanding of the being in question. Every monism is ultimately nihilistic.

Procrustes de Chardin

Another grave philosophical error is closely linked to Teilhard's conception of man; namely, his failure to grasp the radical difference between spirit and matter. Teilhard deals with energy as though it were a genus, and then proceeds to make matter and spirit two *differentiae specificae* of this genus. But there is no genus, energy. Energy is a concept that is applicable to both of these radically different realms of being only in terms of analogy. Teilhard did not understand this; he even speaks of the "spiritual power of matter."

Teilhard, then, is the type of thinker who indulges in constructions and hypotheses without caring much about what is "given." Maritain once said: "The main difference between philosophers is whether they see or do not see." In Teilhard, there is much imagination but no intuition, no listening to experience. Thus Teilhard's attempt to project consciousness into inanimate matter; there is simply no foundation for it apart from his desire to erect a monistic system. Instead of listening to the voice of being in experience, he arbitrarily infuses into the being in question whatever corresponds to his system. It is indeed surprising that a man who attacks traditional philosophy and theology for abstractness and for trying to adjust reality to a closed system should himself attempt to force reality into the most abstract and unrealistic system imaginable.

The incongruity of Teilhard's thought also emerges when he accuses communism of being too materialistic, of striving only for the progress of matter, thereby ignoring spiritual progress. His admirers might call this proof that Teilhard clearly distinguished between matter and spirit and acknowledged the superiority of the latter. Actually, it proves no such thing. Teilhard always distinguishes between matter and spirit, but he regards them as merely two stages in the evolutionary process. Physical energy becomes—is transformed into—a spiritual energy. But to regard the difference between the two as simply stages of a process —or, as we may put it, to regard the difference as a "gradual" one—is to fail utterly to understand the nature of the spirit. Again, monism bars an understanding of reality, and creates the illusion of being able to combine what cannot be combined.

Free Will Denied

Teilhard's incomprehension of man's nature again comes to the fore in his implicit denial of man's free will. "The moral and social development of humanity," he says, "is certainly the authentic and 'natural' consequence of organic evolution." By grounding man's spiritual life in an evolutionary process—which, by definition, acts independently of man's free will and transcends the person—Teilhard clearly denies the decisive role of human freedom. Thus, once again, he overlooks the radical difference between man, as person, and a highly developed animal; freedom of the will is obviously one of the most significant and deepest marks of a person.

Backward to Omega

The role of free will emerges decisively in man's capacity to bear moral values and disvalues. For this highest characteristic of man presupposes free will and responsibility. But Teilhard blithely reduces the antithesis between good and evil to mere stages of evolution, to more degrees of perfection—surely a classic case of philosophical impotence. Moreover, he ignores the critical importance of the moral question, which is strikingly expressed in Socrates' immortal dictum: "It is better for man to suffer injustice than to commit it." In Teilhard, the entire drama of man's existence, the fight between good and evil in his soul, is ignored, or rather overshadowed by the evolutionary growth toward the Omega.

Teilhard's thought is thus hopelessly at odds with Christianity.

Christian revelation presupposes certain basic natural facts, such as the existence of objective truth, the spiritual reality of an individual person, the radical difference between spirit and matter, the difference between body and soul, the unalterable objectivity of moral good and evil, freedom of will, the immortality of the soul—and of course, the existence of a personal God. Teilhard's approach to all of these questions reveals an unbridgeable chasm between his theology-fiction and Christian revelation.

This conclusion is inescapable when listening to Teilhard's oft-repeated arguments for a "new" interpretation of Christianity. Time and again he argues that we can no longer expect modem man, living in an industrialized world and in the scientific age, to accept Christian doctrine as it has been taught for the last 2,000 years. Teilhard's new interpretation of Christianity is fashioned by asking, "What fits into our modern world?" This approach combines historical relativism and pragmatism with a radical blindness to the very essence of religion. Mere historical relativism confuses the sociohistorical "aliveness" of an idea, on the one hand, and its validity and truth on the other. But if it is sheer nonsense to assert that a basic natural truth might be valid for the Middle Ages but no longer be so in our epoch, the absurdity becomes even more drastic when the subject is religion.

Man always remains essentially the same regarding his moral dangers, his moral obligations, his need of redemption and the true sources of his happiness.

With a religion the only question that can matter is whether or not it is true. The question of whether or not it fits into the mentality of an epoch cannot play any role in the acceptance or the rejection of a religion without betraying the very essence of religion. Even the earnest atheist recognizes this. He will not say that today we can no longer believe in God; he will say that God is and always was a mere illusion. From the position that a religion must be adapted to the spirit of an epoch there is but a short step to the absurd drivel about having to invent a new religion which we associate with Bertrand Russell or the Nazi ideologist Bergmann.

Forward from God

Teilhard wrote in a letter in 1952: "As I love to say, the synthesis of the Christian God (of the above), and the Marxist

God (of the forward), behold that is the Only God whom henceforth we can adore in spirit and in truth." In this sentence the abyss separating Teilhard from Christianity is manifest in every word. To speak of a Marxist God is very surprising to say the least, and would never have been accepted by Marx. But the idea of a synthesis of the Christian God with an alleged Marxist God, as well as the simultaneous application of the term God to Christianity and to Marxism, demonstrates the absolute incompatibility of Teilhard's thought with the doctrine of the Church. Note, moreover, the words "henceforth" and "can." They are key to Teilhard's thinking and expose unmistakably his historical relativism.

Deforming the Deposit

In his important book, *The Peasant of the Garonne*, Jacques Maritain remarks that Teilhard is most anxious to preserve Christ. But, Maritain adds, "What a Christ!" Here indeed we find the most radical difference between the doctrine of the Church and Teilhard de Chardin's theology-fiction. Teilhard's Christ is no longer Jesus, the God-man, the epiphany of God, the Redeemer; instead He is the initiator of a purely natural evolutionary process and, simultaneously, its end— the Christ-Omega. An unprejudiced mind cannot but ask: Why should this "cosmic force" be called Christ?

It would be a peak of naiveté to be misled by the mere fact that Teilhard labels this alleged cosmogenic force "Christ," or by his desperate effort to wrap this pantheism in traditional Catholic terms. In his basic conception of the world, which does not provide for original sin in the sense the Church gives to this term, there is no place for the Jesus Christ of the Gospels. For, if there is no original sin, then the redemption of man through Christ loses its inner meaning.

In Christian revelation, the stress is laid on the sanctification and salvation of every individual person, leading to the beatific vision and, simultaneously the communion of saints.

In Teilhard's theology, the stress is laid on the progress of the earth, the evolution leading to Christ-Omega. There is no place for salvation through Christ's death on the Cross, because man's destiny is part of the pancosmic evolution.

Thus Teilhard's conception of man and his implicit denial of free will, his tacit amoralism and his totalitarian collectivism, cut him off from Christian revelation—and this notwithstanding his efforts to reconcile his views with the Church's teaching. He is half aware of this incompatibility: "Sometimes I am a bit afraid, when I think of the transposition to which I must submit my mind concerning the vulgar notions of creation, inspiration, miracle, original sin, resurrection, etc., in order to be able to accept them."

That Teilhard applies the term "vulgar"—even if not in the pejorative sense—to the basic elements of Christian revelation and their interpretation by the infallible magisterium of the Church should suffice to disclose the gnostic and esoteric character of his thought.

Teilhard writes to Leontine Zanta: "As you already know, what dominates my interest and my inner preoccupations is the effort to establish in myself and to spread around a new religion (you may call it a better Christianity) in which the personal God ceases to be the great monolithic proprietor of former times, in order to become the soul of the world; our religious and cultural stage calls for this." Not only, then, is the Christ of the Gospels replaced by a Christ-Omega, but also the God of the old and new covenant is replaced by a pantheistic God, "the soul of the world"—and again on the strength of the unfortunate argument that God must be adapted to the man of our scientific age.

It is no wonder that Teilhard reproaches Saint Augustine for having introduced the difference between the natural and the supernatural. In Teilhard's pantheistic and naturalistic "religion" there is no place for the supernatural or the world of grace. For him, union with God consists principally in assimilation into an evolutionary process—not in the supernatural life of grace which is infused in our souls through baptism. Why does the one tend to exclude the other? If Teilhard's notion of a participation in an evolutionary process were reality, it could only be a form of *concursus divinus*. Yet great and mysterious as the *concursus divinus* is—i.e., the support God gives at every moment of our natural existence, without which we would sink back into nothingness—an abyss separates this *natural* metaphysical contact from grace. Whether or not Teilhard explicitly denies the reality of grace does not much matter: his ecstasy in the presence of the natural contact with God in the alleged evolutionary process clearly discloses the subordinate role, if any, that he assigns to grace.

Or, put otherwise: having replaced the personal God, Creator of heaven and earth, by God, the soul of the world; having transformed the Christ of the Gospels into the Christ-Omega; having replaced redemption by a natural evolutionary process, what is *left* for grace?

Maritain makes the point admirably in *The Peasant of the Garonne*. Having granted that Teilhard's spectacle of a divine movement of creation toward God does not lack grandeur, Maritain observes: "... but what does he tell us about the secret path which matters more for us than any spectacle? What can he tell us about the essential, the Mystery of the Cross, and the redeeming blood as well as of the grace whose presence in one single soul has more worth than all of nature? And what about this love which makes us co-redeemers with Christ, and of these blissful tears through which His peace enters into our soul? The new gnosis is, like all other gnoses, 'a poor gnosis.' "

In Teilhard we find a complete reversal of the Christian hierarchy of values: for him, cosmic processes rank higher than the individual soul. Research and work rank higher than moral values. Action as such—that is, any association with the evolutionary process—is more important than contemplation, contrition for our sins and penance. Progress in the conquest and totalization of the world through evolution ranks higher than holiness. The abyss separating Teilhard's world from the Christian one becomes clear when we compare Cardinal Newman with Teilhard.

Newman says in *Discourses to Mixed Congregations:*

> Saintly purity, saintly poverty, renouncement of the world, the flavor of Heaven, the protection of the angels, the smile of the blessed Mary, the gifts of grace, the interposition of miracles, the intercommunion of merits, these are the high and precious things, the things to be looked up to, the things to be reverently spoken of.

Teilhard says:

> To adore once meant to prefer God to things by referring them to Him and by sacrificing them to Him. Adoring today becomes giving oneself body and soul to the creator—associating ourselves with the creator—in order to give the finishing touch to the world through work and research.

Teilhard's ambiguous use of classical Christian terms will never lead a man with a *sensus supranaturalis* to misunderstand him. Such a man can never conclude with Henri de Lubac that his theology-fiction is a "possible" addition to

Christian revelation. Rather, he will agree with Philippe de la Trinité that it is "a deformation of Christianity, which is transformed into an evolutionism of the naturalistic, monistic and pantheistic brand."

A peculiar confusion reigns in Teilhard's writings, a gliding from one notion into another—a cult of equivocation which is deeply linked to his monistic ideal. He systematically blurs all the decisive differences between things: for instance, the difference between hope and optimism, and between Christian love of neighbor (which is essentially directed to an individual person) and an infatuation for humanity. And Teilhard ignores the difference between eternity and an earthly future for humanity, both of which he fuses in the totalization of the Christ-Omega.

To be sure, there is something touching in Teilhard's desperate attempt to combine a traditional, emotional attraction to the Church with a theology radically opposed to the Church's doctrine. But this apparent dedication to Christian terms makes him even more dangerous than a Voltaire, a Renan or a Nietzsche. His success in wrapping a pantheistic, gnostic monism in Christian garments is perhaps nowhere so evident as in *The Divine Milieu.*

To many readers, the terms Teilhard uses sound so familiar that they can exclaim: How can you accuse him of not being an orthodox Christian? Does he not say in *The Divine Milieu,* "What is it for a person to be a saint if not, in effect, to adhere to God with all his power?" Certainly this sounds absolutely orthodox. Actually, however, Teilhard's notion of adhering to God conceals a shift from the heroic virtues that characterize the saint to a collaboration in an evolutionary process. The significance of attaining holiness in the moral sphere, of obeying God's commands, of imitating Christ is tacitly replaced by emphasis on developing all of man's faculties with, for lack of a better word, efficiency.

Teilhard makes this clear, although he veils the point in traditional terminology:

> ...and what is it to adhere to God to the maximum if not to fulfill in the world organized around Christ the exact function, humble or important, to which nature and supernature destines it?

For Teilhard, then, the very meaning of the individual person lies in his fulfillment of a function in the whole—in the evolutionary process; he is no longer called upon to glorify God through imitation of Christ, which is the one common goal for every true Christian.

The transposition of the Cross into the Christ-Omega is also wrapped in apparently traditional terms:

> Towards the summits veiled to our human eyes where we carry the crucifix we raise ourselves up by the way of universal progress, the royal way of the Cross—that is the route of human effort, supernaturally ordered and extended.

Here we can see that Christian symbols conceal a radical transformation of Christianity that takes us out of the Christian orbit altogether into a completely different climate. Sometimes, however, Teilhard does discard the Christian guise, and openly reveals his true stand. In 1934, he wrote:

> If in consequence of some inner revolution, I were to lose my faith in Christ, my faith in a personal God, my faith in the spirit, it seems to me that I would continue to have faith in the world. The world (the value, infallibility and goodness of the world) this is—definitely—the first and only thing in which I believe.

Yet, clear as the heterodoxy of Teilhard's theology is, some Catholics have elevated him to the rank of a Doctor, indeed, even a Father of the Church. For many unsophisticated Catholics, he has become a kind of prophet.

That "progressive" Catholics relish Teilhard is, of course, not surprising. The "new" theologians, the "new" moralists, welcome Teilhard's views because they share his historical relativism—his conviction that faith must be adapted to "modern man." Indeed for many "progressive" Catholics, Teilhard's transformation of Christian revelation does not go far enough. But it is astonishing, on the other hand, that many faithful Christians are carried away—that they fail to grasp the utter incompatibility of Teilhard's teaching with the doctrine of the Church.

This popularity becomes less surprising when viewed in the context of our contemporary intellectual and moral climate. In a period familiar with Heidegger's conception of the essentially "homeless" man and Sartre's "nausea," Teilhard's radiant and optimistic outlook on life comes for many as a welcome relief. His claim that we are constantly collaborating with God, whatever we do and however insignificant our role—that everything is "sacred"—understandably exhilarates many depressed souls. Another reason for such enthusiasm, perhaps more important, is that Teilhard is credited with having overcome a narrow asceticism and false supernaturalism.

There is no doubt that in the past many pious Catholics considered natural goods primarily as potential dangers that threatened to divert them from God. Natural goods, even those endowed with high values—beauty in nature and in art, natural truth and human love—were approached with suspicion. These Catholics overlooked the positive value that natural goods have for man. They frequently advocated the view that natural goods should only be *used*, that they should never evoke interest and appreciation for their own sake. But in this view they forgot the fundamental difference between *natural* goods and *worldly* goods, such as wealth, fame or success. They forgot that natural goods, endowed with intrinsic value, should not only be "used," but appreciated for their own sake—that it was worldly goods that should be "used" only.

It cannot be denied, moreover, that this unfortunate oversimplification often gained currency in seminaries and monasteries, notwithstanding that it was never part of the doctrine of the Church. This is why Teilhard is able, with superficial plausibility, to accuse the Catholic tradition of disparaging nature; and because he himself praises nature, it is understandable that for many his thought has seemed to be a just appreciation of natural goods.

Teilhard's related claim that traditional Christianity has created a gap between humanness and Christian perfection has also impressed many sincere Catholics. In *The Divine Milieu* he attributes to traditional Christianity the notion that: "men must put off their human garments in order to be Christians." Again, it cannot be denied that Jansenism reflects this attitude, or that Jansenist tendencies have crept anonymously into the minds of many Catholics. For instance, the arch-Christian doctrine which insists that we must die to ourselves in order to be transformed in Christ has often been given an unwarranted dehumanizing emphasis in certain religious institutions. The view has been encouraged in some monasteries and seminaries that nature must, in effect, be killed before the supernatural life of grace can blossom. In the official doctrine of the Church, however, such dehumanization is flatly rejected. As Pope Pius XII said: "Grace does not destroy nature; it does not even change it; it tranfigures it. Indeed, dehumanization is so far from being required for Christian perfection that this may be said: only the person who is transformed in Christ embodies the true fulfillment of his human personality."

What matters here is that Teilhard himself ignores the value of high natural goods, and that, contrary to his claim, a real dehumanization *does* take place in his monistic pantheism. We have seen that his ideal of collective man and superhumanity necessarily rests upon a blindness to the real nature of the individual person and, derivatively, to all the plenitude of human life. But dehumanization also follows inevitably from his monism, which minimizes the real drama of human life—the fight between good and evil—and which reduces antithetical differences to the merely gradual ones of a continuum.

Teilhard's failure to do justice to the real significance of natural goods becomes clear at the very moment he stresses their importance for eternity. In dealing with natural goods he is primarily concerned with human activities, with accomplishments in work and research. He does not mention the higher natural goods and the message of God they contain, but only activities, performances and accomplishments in the natural field.

Teilhard applies to these actions the biblical words *"opera ejus sequuntur illos"*; but he does so in contradistinction to the original meaning of *opera*, in which "works" are identical with *morally significant deeds*. Still more important is the relation he sees between natural goods as such and God. Teilhard sees no message of God's glory in the values contained in these great natural goods; nor does he find in them a personal experience of the voice of God. Instead, he posits an objective and unexperienced link between God and our activities, resulting from the *concursus divinus*. He says: "God is, in a way, at the end of my pen, of my pickax, of my paintbrush, of my sewing needle, of my heart, of my thought."

The real object of Teilhard's boundless enthusiasm, then, is not natural goods themselves, but an abstraction: the hypothesis of evolution. The nature that moves him is not the colorful, sounding beauty of which all the great poets sing. It is not the nature of Dante, Shakespeare, Keats, Goethe, Hoelderlin, Leopardi. It is not the glory of a sunrise or sunset, or the star-studded sky—the evidences of the natural world which Kant regarded, along with the moral law in man's breast, as the most sublime thing of all.

There is another way in which Teilhard's thought necessarily results in a dehumanization of the cosmos and man's life. In his world view there is no place for an antithesis of values and disvalues. Yet every attempt to deny these ultimately important qualitative antagonisms always produces a kind of leveling, even a nihilism. The same thing happens when the *hierarchy* of values is overlooked, if only because man responds at all levels of value with the same degree of enthusiasm.

The principle "everything is sacred," which sounds so uplifting and exhilarating, is in reality fraught with a nihilistic denial of low and high, of good and evil. This fallacious and treacherous approach of praising everything actually results in denying everything. It reminds me of a remark made by a violinist I once met. "I love music so much," he said, "that I do not care what kind of music it is, granted that it is music." This statement, meant to signify an extraordinary love for music, in fact revealed an absence of any true understanding of music, and thus of any capacity really to love music.

The same thing happens to man when qualitative distinctions are not made.

The revelation of God in nature has always been affirmed by the Christian tradition. The *Sanctus* says, *"pleni sunt caeli et terra gloria tua."* The Psalms are filled with praise of God,

199

as the Creator of nature and all of its marvelous features. Saint Augustine's exemplarism emphasizes time and again the message of God in the beauty of nature. The same idea is found in Saint Francis' love of nature.

But an appreciation of this natural revelation of God implies an "upward direction to God," to use Teilhard's terminology. Natural revelation speaks to us of God by suggesting the admirable wisdom that pervades creation; and by providing a reflection, in the values of natural goods, of God's infinite beauty and glory. Our response to this revelation is either trembling reverence and wonder for the wisdom manifest in the finality of the cosmos and its mysterious plenitude—a looking up to God the Creator; or, at least, a deep awareness of the beauty of nature and of all the high natural goods—which also lifts up our vision. In either case, we are able to grasp the message from above: that all true values are pregnant with a promise of eternity. By lifting up our hearts we are able to understand that these authentic values speak of God's infinite glory. All of this unmistakably implies an "upward direction."

But Teilhard's "nature" is not linked to an "upward direction"; it is not a message from above. Since God, for Teilhard, is *behind* nature, we are supposed to reach Him in the Christ-Omega by moving in a "forward direction."

In Teilhard's forward direction, where everything is involved in an evolutionary movement, natural goods lose their real value. Their suggestion of something transcendent is replaced by a merely immanent finality, by becoming a link in the chain of evolution. When evolution is viewed as the main and decisive reality—is, in fact, deified—then every natural good becomes, on the one hand, a mere transitory step in the forward movement of the evolutionary process; and, on the other, a mute, dumb thing, cut off by a leveling monism from its real, qualitative, inherent importance.

It follows that we can do justice to high natural goods only if we discern in them a reflection of an infinitely higher reality—a reality ontologically different from them. This "message character" of natural goods is admirably expressed in Cardinal Newman's remarks about music.

> Can it be that those mysterious stirrings of the heart, and keen emotion, and strange yearnings after we know not what, and awful impressions from we know not whence, should be brought in us by what is unsubstantial, and comes and goes, and begins and ends in itself? It is not so; it cannot be. No; they have escaped from some higher sphere, they are the outpourings of eternal harmony in the medium of created sound; they are echoes of our home; they are the voice of angels, or the Magnificat of the Saints.....

Another aspect of this problem deserves notice. The fact that Teilhard sees a higher stage of evolution in today's industrialized world reveals the lack of a real sense for the beauty of nature and for the qualitative message of God that it bears. Even the most enthusiastic "progressive" cannot deny that industrialization consistently ruins the beauty of nature. Industrialization, moreover, (though perhaps the process is inevitable) certainly cannot be considered a universal blessing, from the point of view either of increasing human happiness, or of fostering higher culture or a real humanism. As Gabriel Marcel correctly shows in his *Man Against Mass Society*, industrialization implies the danger of a progressive dehumanization. The replacing of the "organic" in human life by the artificial—from artificial insemination to social engineering—is symptomatic of this dehumanization. Yet Teilhard heedlessly jumps from an enthusiasm for nature to elation over the progress of technology and industrialization. We are again confronted with his blindness to antitheses, with his monistic leveling.

It is clear, nevertheless, that Teilhard's first love is technological progress. The creation of God has to be completed by man—not in St. Paul's sense, not in a cooperation with nature, but by replacing nature with the machine.

Teilhard's poetic expressions, as when he speaks of his vision of evolution and progress, make clear that he never saw the authentic poetry of nature, or of the classical "forms" of creation. Instead, he tries to project poetry into technology—again revealing a monistic denial of the basic differences between the poetic and the prosaic, the organic and the artificial, the sacred and the profane.

To be sure, it is always impressive when a man seems to have achieved a deep vision of being, and, instead of taking it for granted, gives it a full and ardent response. So with Teilhard. We are far from denying that he discerned in matter many aspects which had generally been overlooked. For example, the mysterious structure and the multiplicity of matter, which natural science is increasingly unfolding, call for genuine wonderment about this reality, and for respect for this creation of God. But because Teilhard does not recognize the essential difference between spirit and matter— because his response to the spirit is not in proportion to his praise of matter (recall his "prayer" to matter)—the advantage of this unusual insight into matter is, for him, quickly lost.

We must put this question of "matter" in its proper perspective. To overlook the marvels hidden in a creature that ranks lowest in the hierarchy of being is regrettable. But the oversight does not affect our knowledge of higher ranking creatures; it is therefore not a catastrophe. On the other hand, to grasp the lower while overlooking the higher is to distort our entire world view; and that is a catastrophe. Moreover, to esteem a lower good as a higher is to misunderstand the hierarchical structure of being, and thus to lose the basis for properly evaluating either higher things or lower things.

Teilhard's blindness to the real values in, for example, human love is shown in these unfortunate remarks about *eros* and *agape:*

> Naturally, I agree with you that the solution of the eros-agape problem is simply to be found in the evolutionary trend *(dans l'evolutif),* in the genetic, that is to say, in sublimation....[It is to be found in] the spirit emerging from matter through the pancosmic operation.....

We have already seen that Teilhard's conception of the moral sphere (virtue and sin) is incompatible with Christian revelation. We may now note that the role he grants to the moral sphere is yet another factor leading to dehumanization.

The unique contact with God which takes place in one's conscience, in one's awareness of his moral obligations, plays no role in Teilhard's system. He does not understand that man, in the realm of nature, never reaches so intimate a contact with God as when he listens to the voice of his conscience and consciously submits to moral obligation. How pale by comparison—in purely human and natural terms—is Teilhard's notion of the "conscious" and the "unconscious" participation in a "cosmic progress"!

And how pale are the scope and breadth of cosmic events in contrast with the liberating transcendence of a man authentically contrite. What event could hold more grandeur than David's response to the challenge of the prophet Nathan? The secondary role which Teilhard assigns to man's conscious and personal dialogue with Christ—his preference for objective cooperation in the "evolutionary process" reveals as clearly as anything can the truly dehumanized character of his "new world."

Many people are impressed by a thinker who constructs a new world out of his own mind, a world in which everything is interconnected and "explained." They consider such conceptions the most eminent feat of the human mind; accordingly, they praise Teilhard as a great synthetic thinker. In truth, however, the measure of a thinker's greatness is the extent to which he has grasped reality in its plenitude and depth, and in its hierarchical structure. If *this* measure is applied to Teilhard, he obviously cannot be considered a great thinker.

These reflections may be concluded with two quotations. Teilhard wrote:

> [Christ] becomes the flame of human efforts, he reveals himself as the form of faith which is most appropriate for modern needs—a religion for progress, the religion even for progress on earth; I dare say: the religion of evolution.

Cardinal Newman wrote:

> The Church aims, not at making a show, but at doing a work. She regards this world, and all that is in it, as a mere shadow, as dust and ashes, compared with the value of one single soul. She holds that unless she can, in her own way, do good to souls, it is no use her doing anything....She considers the action of this world and the action of the soul simply incommensurate, viewed in their respective spheres; she would rather save the soul of one single wild bandit of Calabria, or whining beggar of Palermo, than draw a hundred lines of railroad through the length and breadth of Italy, or of Sicily,

except so far as these great national works tended to some spiritual good beyond them.

Which of these observations echoes the message of Christ?

Index

Index

Sources

Each of the 20 essays comprising this book was originally delivered as an address to the Roman Forum, which met regularly at Fordham University in the Bronx, N.Y., in the late 1960s and early 1970s, under the auspices of Professors Dietrich von Hildebrand and William A. Marra. The addresses were then submitted as essays to *Triumph* and *The Wanderer*.